'Gotcha'

'Gotcha'

✦

International Marine Insurance Fraud and Conspiracy

A study guide

Ed Geary

50% of the people are honest
   25% are dishonest....
      The remaining 25% are as honest as the system they work under.
                                                              —*Anon...*

iUniverse, Inc.
New York Lincoln Shanghai

'Gotcha'
International Marine Insurance Fraud and Conspiracy

iUniverse, Inc.

For information address:
iUniverse, Inc.
2021 Pine Lake Road, Suite 100
Lincoln, NE 68512
www.iuniverse.com

ISBN: 0-595-32740-0

Printed in the United States of America

This book is dedicated to the memory of the late
Myles Jay Tralins.

Myles was born in Baltimore, Maryland on August 23, 1947 and was admitted to the Florida Bar in 1971. He practiced international and corporate law from his office in Miami and was my counselor, confidant, mentor and most important, my friend. After preparing his new yacht in Plymouth, England for a voyage to the 2004 Olympics, and while driving on the M4 to London's Heathrow airport, he was tragically killed in an automobile accident on Monday, May 17, 2004. Myles was admired and will be missed by everyone who knew him. He may be gone but will not be forgotten. In spite of his earthly absence, all those who knew him and cherished his friendship will have the consolation that if there is a body of water in heaven, Myles will soon be hoisting the sails and simply continuing on another voyage into eternity. Bon Voyage my friend, may you always have following seas with fair winds and full sails.

Contents

Introduction

There are times when it is better to seek forgiveness......
than to first ask permission.

After a number of years being involved in the marine insurance field I have lived and personally experienced what you are about to read. I hope you will find it interesting, entertaining and to some, educationally relevant. As knowledge is a powerful tool in life's endeavors, irrespective of the profession or field, it is imperative that one strive to expand and continually increase their educational levels for personal satisfaction and for the benefit of those we serve. Being raised as a Catholic I was fortunate to have the benefit of counsel from dedicated priests, who were also members of my immediate family which meant that my Sermons weren't only limited to Sunday Mass. While it would not be angelic to claim to have been the model choir boy as prayed for by my family, I was regularly exposed to righteous principles and values that provided me with the insight to recognize right from wrong at an early age. Learning begins when you are born and only ends when you die. Through education one develops knowledge, from knowledge comes perception which improves with experience, from experience we gain wisdom. While I may have developed and contributed to the equation of knowledge, perception, experience and wisdom I could not have achieved any level of success without the backing, support and confidence of the numerous individual underwriters, insurance companies, banks, lawyers and private clients who demonstrated their trust and relied on my professional expertise. However, I feel it's only appropriate to begin by saying that there will be a number of those who may be displeased when they recognize themselves as one of the clowns, self-absorbed snobs, weasels and fraudsters to which I will also refer. As to the weasels, while I may not exactly agree with everything he puts forth I believe that Bill O'Reilly provided an accurate and colorful description of a weasel in his recent book *Who's Looking Out For You*. **"Weasels are by nature small carnivores that hunt alone at night, in the dark, and viciously kill their weaker prey. There are legions of human weasels in America (and in marine insurance in other parts of the world—my annexation) today. They have dens where they hang out with other weasels. But if you are not one of them, they don't want you in the den. And believe me; you don't want to be there, because if there is just one morsel of weasel food, it will not be shared. The strongest weasel will take it, and the other weasels will starve. There are no socialist weasels."**

Good Guys, Bad Guys and the Weasels

The Insurance Industry has them all

One excellent example of a weasel would be Tony Button who operated the Sint Maarten Insurance Agency in the Netherlands Antilles. Over a long period of time Button sold yacht insurance policies to the owners of large high value private yachts as well as charter boats operating in the French and Dutch West Indies and in the British Virgin Islands. The owners of these yachts paid their premiums and were issued Cover Notes under the name LLOYD'S OF LONDON. Unfortunately as Button hadn't placed the insurance with Lloyd's Underwriters or paid them the premiums, they weren't aware of the cover notes. Business was good and Button's fortunes increased substantially until Hurricane Luis struck the Eastern Caribbean on September 9th 1995. On behalf of Dutch, German and London underwriters I assembled a Catastrophic Response Team and we proceeded to the effected islands to deal with over 250 marine claims. There is no way that I could adequately describe the destruction and human tragedy that I found on the island of Sint Maarten. Those living aboard their boats had lost their homes and at least one wife was tasked to bury her dead husband. Children were traumatized in prolonged winds that exceeded 200 miles per hour, there was no power, no water and food was in short supply. Day and night the CAT TEAM (catastrophic response team) worked to locate boats that had sunk or were piled high in corners of the Simpson Bay Lagoon or in some cases had been blown to neighboring islands. Knowing of my presence on the island I received a number of messages by VHF radio (which was the only form of communication) from a number of yacht owners asking if I could deal with their claims that had been covered under Lloyd's of London policies issued by Tony Button of Sint Maarten Insurance. To keep the lines of communication open with underwriters, every three days I was traveling back to my office in Puerto Rico to update the claims assignments but found no claims for the vessels reportedly insured through Sint Maarten Insurance. In returning to Sint Maarten I was overwhelmed by an increasing number of yacht owners who believing they were insured with syndicates at Lloyd's, demanded that I deal with their claims because they couldn't find Tony Button.

In an effort to find out what the status was I took one of the Cover Notes issued by Button with me on my return trip to Puerto Rico and faxed it to London. I then learned that the Cover Notes issued by Button in the name of Lloyd's of London were bogus. Underwriters quickly reported the fraud to the authorities. Button had issued an unknown number of fraudulent Cover Notes and then simply pocketed the premiums. Before Hurricane Luis hit the Caribbean, Button had gotten away with his scheme to defraud various yacht owners by personally paying a number of small claims to avoid any suspicion. Everything worked fine until the islands were impacted by a major hurricane that brought on huge losses. One of his bogus non-marine policies had been issued to a hotel and casino on the Dutch side of the island that was owned and operated by a MAFIA family. The property had been damaged to the tune of US$10M.; in an effort to have their claim settled promptly the hotel management brought in two rather nasty family members from New York that were aggressively attempting to locate Mr. Button. On my return to San Juan, Puerto Rico with American Airlines, I found the San Juan airport had been closed due to storm damage. American put me on a flight through

Miami, advising that the following day I could return to San Juan as the airport was scheduled to be back in operation. After boarding the plane to Miami I saw Tony Button moving towards the first class cabin with what seemed like all his personal belongings in five pieces of carry-on. I approached him and asked why he was leaving when literally dozens of his policyholders were trying to find him? His answer was that he was going to New York to pick up the cash to pay his claims. Yeah Right. Underwriters don't pay claims in cash and don't give currency to retail agents for any reason. Caught in a blatant fraud Button was clearly escaping the nightmare he had created for himself. After reaching Miami I watched Button as he beat a hasty retreat from the plane. Following him at a reasonable distance through concourse D he frequently glanced over his shoulder while making his way to the American Airlines Admirals Club. After waiting a few minutes I too took the elevator and entered the Club just as Button was moving away from the concierge desk. I asked the receptionist if by chance my friend Tony Button had checked in for the flight to New York. She said that indeed Mr. Button had just checked in, not for New York, but on the flight to Toronto. So as not to attract his suspicion I left the Club and at the closest pay phone I made a call to my colleagues at INTERPOL to report that Button was enroute to Toronto. The Canadian RCMP took a number of weeks to track Button down, but he was subsequently arrested and charged.

While we're on the subject of weasels it's only appropriate to mention the Dome Insurance Company of Christiansted on St. Croix in the U.S. Virgin Islands. One afternoon in the early 1980's I received a call from a Philip Bloom who represented himself as one of the owners of Dome Insurance. Phil said he was aware of my experience with marine insurance in the West Indies and in particular policy wording, coverage issues and claims. He said they had a great deal of experience in property and casualty but would like to retain me as a consultant to help them with their entry into the marine market. Being flattered by the call and humbled by the prospects I was soon on my way to Christiansted. Phil was a charming guy in his mid-thirties that at first appeared knowledgeable. He said that

Dome's operations were based in St. Croix, but that the corporation's chairman Leo Bloom, his father, was presently located in Pennsylvania. When I inquired about corporate structure, security for the policies and reinsurance he responded that the company had four million dollars on deposit at a bank on the island of Anguilla and that he was in the process of negotiating reinsurance treaties in Zurich and London. Phil said that he would be grateful if I might review their policy wording and suggest any changes to their corporate counsel, establish a claims procedure and paper work trail for use in-house and by their retail agents, which he said had been established on a number of Caribbean islands. In return I would be placed on a generous monthly retainer. The work soon began in earnest with the creation of marine policies that were based on standard wording and warranties. Premiums were to be determined based on a percentage of hull value, location, navigational limits and a number of other factors including the deductible. In the event of a claim the assured had the option to select new-for-old, one-thirds off or an annual depreciation of fortuitous losses of the damaged components. As hull and machinery insurance has and continues to be difficult to obtain in the Caribbean area, retail brokers were pleased to have a local market and began selling policies at a brisk rate. In the beginning claims were few and those that were filed were inconsequential. This soon changed. Some larger agents were given the *Pen* (this is where the individual retail insurance agent or broker is given the authority to bind or accept a risk without first submitting it to the company for approval) these agents quickly developed a book of business that was made up of rust buckets and derelicts. Early on I had cautioned Phil about not giving binding authority to anyone as it could ultimately destroy the company. This was the first red flag to appear on the horizon.

It became obvious that the Dome Insurance Company wasn't interested in longevity but wanted only to increase premium income. And increase it did. In a short period of time Dome's premium income sky rocketed to the millions. In the beginning I dealt with a few small claims on Dome's behalf and then was asked to inspect the damages on a cruise ship that had gone aground in Papeete on the island of Tahiti in the South Pacific. The loss appeared to be significant enough for Phil to call me and personally give the instructions. I asked him why in the hell he had insured a 20 year old passenger ship operating half-way around the world, that wasn't even in Class; I also asked what policy wording had been used. His answer was that the owner had paid a large premium and he had just changed a few words on the yacht policy. His parting remark was, "I hope you can get us out of this one!" After 24 hours of traveling I met with the ship's master and learned that the damages were limited only to a light touching of the bottom as he had been passing the reef at Bora-Bora. When I reported back to Dome, Phil was excited to find that the damages were minor and could be repaired during the ship's next dry-docking in 10 months time. This loss was however, a wakeup call to me to take a closer look at what really was behind the Dome Insurance Company. In checking with a friend in Philadelphia I found that Leo Bloom, the chairman of Dome Insurance had indeed been located in Pennsylvania when the company was formed—as an inmate of the federal penitentiary. Leo Bloom was a convicted felon who had recently been released after serving a sentence for insurance fraud. In making some further inquiries through sources in London and in Anguilla I found that Dome's four million dollars security was nothing more than two certificates of deposit issued by a defunct bank in the Bahamas that had been dissolved and placed in receivership. The original retainer that Dome had paid me was quickly depleted for the work I had carried out in the previous months and even though they owed me another $5,000 for the trip to Tahiti, it was clearly time to cut and run. I wrote Phil a withdrawal letter and immediately canceled my professional services agreement. But it wasn't over. A few days later I received a call from the FBI asking for a meeting concerning—you guessed it, Dome Insurance. The FBI agent was a pleasant and very professional individual.

This meant that he smiled a lot before demanding to know exactly what my connection was with Dome and the Blooms. Everyone who was involved with Dome Insurance was in the FBI's sights for possible prosecution. I told him the arrangement was purely as a consultant, I had no shares and no financial interest in Dome in any way. It always pays to tell the truth, as before I stopped speaking, the FBI Agent pulled out a copy of my professional services agreement from his briefcase. He knew exactly what my relationship had been, but was on a fishing trip to see if my connection with Dome went any further. Smiling again the FBI Special Agent assured me he was just checking. In their investigation the FBI found that Phil and Leo Bloom had swindled thousands of policyholders and other business creditors out of millions of dollars during their short existence. Dome had been declared bankrupt and placed under the control of a trustee there were few assets left. I never saw Leo or Phil Bloom again. However, I feel confident that in some part of the world where the regulatory agencies that control insurance companies and financial institutions are as lax as those in the U.S. Virgin Islands at the time, the Blooms will have blossomed another creative insurance scam in an industry they know so well. On the other side of the coin I have had the distinct pleasure and been very fortunate to have been associated with a score of insurance and legal professionals who through varying degrees of education, knowledge and practical experience have provided guidance and mentoring that has proved positive over the last 30 years or so. I belong to a number of professional organizations in the United States, the United Kingdom and Europe that persevere in providing me with continuing education and insight that focus on my endeavors in the maritime field. There is however, one organization that has unquestionably been at the forefront of this learning curve, the Association of Certified Fraud Examiners of Austin, Texas. The founder and chairman is a gentleman by the name of Joseph T. Wells. With a Bachelors Degree in Business Administration (with honors) from the University of Oklahoma he cut his teeth in the world of accounting with Coopers & Lybrand before his appointment in 1972 as a Special Agent of the FBI. His government service ended in 1981 when he left the FBI to form Wells & Associates, a consulting group of criminologists involved with fraud detection and deterrence.

No doubt in an effort to share the wisdom he obtained from his experiences in fraud and to bring greater attention to one of the world's growth industries—White Collar Crime and Fraud—in 1988 he founded the Association of Certified Fraud Examiners, the ACFE. Over the last fourteen years the ACFE has grown to a professional organization with over 28,000 members on six continents in 100 countries with 90 local chapters, who at last count had been involved with over 1,000,000 suspected cases of civil and criminal fraud. Now I can't say with any degree of accuracy whether or not Mr. Wells was a distant relative of the J. Paul Getty or his Clan, but he most certainly has the same business acumen. With a million case investigations passing under the keel (a nautical touch) of the ACFE there was definitely a need, and Wells found it. Without wishing to be politically incorrect the ACFE, unlike some other so-called *professional* organizations have rigid initial academic and professional membership requirements followed by mandated continuing education standards. Since the 1920's when Mr. Ponzi began defrauding his neighbors in the northeastern United States, techniques used to defraud have and will continue to change. The ACFE believes and rightly so, that unless the CFE—Certified Fraud Examiner, keeps current on the methods and procedures employed by the criminal element of our society he or she will not be properly trained or equipped to successfully challenge the Ponzis of the 21st century. When I was certified as a CFE in 1999 it opened the door to new opportunities of training and greatly improved my perspectives in the area of international fraud investigation. I guess as they might say in Texas, when you stop learning it maybe time to put you out to pasture. As we're on the subject of good guys it might be an appropriate time to inject some *kudos* for the other good guys and girls that I've had the pleasure to be associated with. Seven Seas Insurance which is part of the Tropical Shipping family is without a doubt the noble prince in the cargo insurance field. Jim McIntire, *el jefe* and Mike Culpepper *el jefe numero dos*, are both revered equally by their employees, assureds and we humble adjusters. Another of these *noble princes* is British Marine Managers in London. Neville Hall, Head of the Marine Department and Chief Surveyor of British Marine is deserving of admiration for his constructive critiques of my loss prevention reports prepared on commercial vessels that Charles Gunning, the astute British Marine underwriter had placed on risk. And of course I cannot fail to mention the kind and forgiving Ms. Liz Burroughs (Neville's right hand) who, before I computerized my reports had to interpret my disgraceful handwriting. Martyn Sherman, Mike Kelly, Carl Gill, Gerald Hamerston and their co-workers on the claims side of British Marine deserve honorable recognition for always being available when I would call them at any hour seeking guidance with a ship that had been arrested in Surinam or needed help with a suspected consignment of tainted sugar from Mexico. In the north of England one finds the offices of T.L. Dallas probably one of the world leaders in yacht insurance. Tony Usher leads this noble band of Yorkshire men and women aided by his wife Sue, the administrative *guru*. While Tony skillfully deals with the underwriting section, the claims side is handled by Mark Thomas who was trained as a solicitor. Mark most likely began his intensive on-the-job-training in those matters of a maritime nature during the mid 1990's; it was during this same period that I showed him how to decipher the USCG hull ID number, explained the principles of Bernoulli's equation for fluid mechanics and prepared their policy depreciation schedules for use in claims adjustments. Mark later described this to me as the *bad period* whatever that means. In late 2003 I questioned some of their claims practices and to preserve my integrity discontinued the relationship. Onno Brinkman, a former senior claims adjuster for the Fortis Group and Ronald Drupsteen of Kuiper Yacht Insurance in Holland displayed an uncommon knowledge and understanding when dealing with yacht and commercial losses; professionals in every respect, but also were just nice people to work with. I first met Erik den Drijver Managing Director of DEN DRIJVER EXPERTS of Amsterdam at a meeting of the International Association of Marine Investigators in New Orleans in the early part of 1991. Even though the top man in his organization, Erik demonstrated a hands-on approach to claim investigations and had no problem with crawling around a smelly and greasy bilge if that's what was needed to find the truth. In the course of the many cases we have worked on together we became close friends while at the same time separating the fraudsters from the good guys. Over the years Erik has demonstrated and uncommon skill and settled hundreds of valid claims while effectively identifying those of felonious intent. Marine insurance is little more than gambling but even the most skilled and proficient gambler occasionally loses with an imprudent bet—or in this case in accepting a bad risk. As I mentioned previously 50% of the people are honest, 25% dishonest and the remaining 25% are as honest as the system they work under. There are a number of cases where a legitimate loss occurs and the insurer settles the claim promptly in accordance with the terms and conditions of the policy—these are the 50% that are honest. Then there are those claims that are submitted with the sole purpose to defraud insurers—the 25% that are dishonest. The remainder of these assureds may begin with a legitimate loss, but are encouraged and tempted by devious repairers to inflate the damages and become influenced by greed are the 25% that are as honest as the system they are controlled by.

Marine Insurance...

The Maze

It may even confuse me at times, but let's take a look at the intricacies and the maze of how the London marine insurance market interacts with the United States and the rest of the maritime world. London is what is known as an alien surplus line market and each individual underwriter must be licensed in every U.S. state he intends to conduct business. In order for surplus lines business to be placed or shall we say, exported from the United States to the London market, it must be either exempt from surplus lines laws or the business has been declined by three U.S. admitted markets. What exactly is a Surplus Line? This is the amount of reinsurance required after having declared the maximum line on a treaty or cover. In the United States it also refers to risks which the producing broker is unable to place with companies resident in his own state and for which he must therefore make arrangements outside the State. In these States it is obligatory by law that the business must first be offered to Companies within the State. As an example, Mr. or Ms. Boat owner approaches a local retail agent say in Florida in an effort to purchase insurance on his or her new $2m yacht, the retail broker would then seek quotes from admitted insurance carriers that they have agency status with. If the business is declined and we assume that this business fits the normal requirements of an admitted market the retail agent would then approach a wholesaler or surplus lines broker. Assuming that three admitted carriers have declined the risk (and the surplus lines broker must have this documented in their files) they are now free to approach the surplus lines market in other States, London or Europe. While there is a substantial surplus lines market in the United States many surplus lines brokers feel that London, because of its experience, is the best and most competitive market for marine risks. On behalf of the retail insurance agent the surplus lines broker would approach a Lloyd's broker to obtain a quote (the quote contains the terms and conditions that would attach to the policy). Between the two parties, the assured and the underwriters, there may be a number of agents and brokers. There are instances where as many as five intermediaries may be involved when surplus lines brokers and Lloyd's brokers do not have direct access to certain underwriters.

Basically it boils down to a boat owner wanting to obtain insurance on his new $2m yacht. His insurance agent tells him that say BoatUS or Progressive don't insure vessels of this size or value or cannot offer navigational limits that include say the Caribbean or anywhere outside of the continental United States. The insurance agent then attempts to place the risk with a number of other companies who also decline the coverage. The agent would then contact a surplus lines broker who has access to insurers in the United Kingdom or Europe who will accept yachts of this value and can provide cover, and the worldwide navigational limits; the yacht owner is then able to obtain the insurance cover he requires. Once the risk has been placed with the underwriter the Lloyd's broker will issue a cover note to the surplus lines broker who will typically issue a certificate of insurance to the assured. Each insurance agent, producer, surplus lines broker and intermediaries are entitled to a piece of the pie (the premium) **if** the underwriter accepts the risk and every marine policy is deemed a 'risk'. The typical commission on a marine policy usually is about 20% which s divided between the Lloyd's brokers, the surplus lines broker and the retail insurance broker. However, in today's market it is not uncommon to find that a percentage of the premium the assured pays for his insurance may be artificially inflated by the retail broker and is gobbled up in the *food chain* as it flows towards the underwriter who ultimately accepts the risk. The practice of premium inflation is known as *Grossing-Up*. To artificially inflate a premium is illegal and a criminal offense. In the Commonwealth of Puerto Rico a 9% tax is levied on insurance policies, plus a standard Policy Fee of $25.00. On a premium of say $2,500.00 the tax would be approximately $225.00. Reputable insurance agents provide an invoice detailing the charges i.e., $2,500.00 for the premium, $225.00 in taxes and the $25.00 policy creation fee—total $2,750.00. Devious agents simply send a lump sum, invoice *inclusive of all charges* for say $3,000.00, pay the taxes and pocket the difference. This is an example of *grossing-up*. In return for the commission paid to the insurance agent, broker and layers of intermediaries the policy holder is supposed to receive professional advice along with guidance, assistance and service in the event of a claim. Don't bet on it! The courts have ruled that insurance agents are agents of the assured and NOT the agent of the insurers. What your insurance agent does is in your name not that of the insurers. It's also important to note that insurance brokers do not have any responsibility or financial liability in the settlement of claims. These same brokers, while they profess to be interested in providing a good service to their clients, and some do, most are interested primarily in the premium income. In this quest for increased income it is not uncommon to find insurance brokers who will dump substandard and unseaworthy vessels on unsuspecting insurers. In the United States Boat/ US has been the leader in a growing number of insurance brokers that after experiencing a number of serious losses by their members, have become wiser and more worldly in programs to educate and inform their members, underwriters and claims people on coverage issues and how to read and understand marine surveys. I first met Richard Swartz (don't ever call him Dick) at the 1992 U.S. Coast Guard Auxiliary conference in San Francisco. I was heading the delegation of the Venezuelan Coastguard Auxiliary and Richard was there as the chairman of BoatUS and a strong supporter of the US Coast Guard Auxiliary. Over the years BoatUS has demonstrated that it is unquestionably at the forefront in boating education, insurance and legislative support for its ever expanding membership.

During my career in addition to meeting Richard Swartz I had the distinct pleasure to know and work with William (Bill) Oakerson now the co-chairman of the BoatUS organization in Alexandria, Virginia. Bill Oaker-son is a prime example of how the cream of an organization always rises to the top. With unblemished integrity and profound professionalism Rich-ard Swartz and Bill Oakerson have lead BoatUS to the vanguard of the marine industry in the United States. In addition to his exceptional knowledge and keen management skills Bill Oakerson is a gentleman and unusually nice guy. If you are fortunate enough to be a BoatUS policy-holder, you're in good hands. My experience in dealing with BoatUS marine claims found them to be responsive, fair and in some cases even generous. On the other hand if you attempt to file a false or fraudulent claim with BoatUS—beware—insurance fraud is a felony and they have no reservations in bringing fraudsters to justice ultimately protecting all the members of the BoatUS organization. Somewhat surprisingly in the United Kingdom and continental Europe old companies that are new to the market have little comprehension of the intricacies of marine insurance and the ridiculous risks they regularly accept. On one occasion when I was in Hamburg discussing the nomenclature of yachts the underwriter some-what seriously, questioned whether the *poop* was only something you picked up after fido's walk. While in Hamburg I called at the offices of a very large marine insurance broker who had a growing book of business in the Mediterranean and the Caribbean. During the visit I found a great group of very knowledgeable people working diligently in the interests of their many clients. One weakness/problem in this particular broker's office was that all the decisions as to claims were being made by a management weasel who had earlier anointed himself a claims specialist. Not particu-larly liking the weather in northern Germany the weasel arranged to set himself up in a pleasant office on the French Mediterranean coast. In spite of having only limited knowledge of yachts or marine insurance in general, the self anointed weasel had been deemed an expert only because of what his co-workers described as his regular bussing of the backside of com-pany's chairman. The weasel was disliked and feared by those in Ham-burg, becoming a force to be reckoned with. No one crossed the weasel. I began dealing with a number of their claims and liked and respected the claims people in Hamburg and considered myself lucky in not having to deal with the weasel, until two years later. The north coast of the Dominican Republic has weather and sea conditions that are inhospitable and which can be outright dangerous for cruising yachts, especially those manned by crews with limited experience. There are only two reasonably safe harbors on the north coast of the Dominican Republic, Puerto Plata and Luperon to the west. One morning I received a fax from the brokers in Hamburg advising that a 42' yacht had taken on water during its voyage from the Turks and Caicos Islands to the Dominican Republic. There were two persons on board, the owner a retired German professor and his son. During a pitch black night at about 2:00 AM water started to enter the boat's interior, the professor's son had quickly stuffed pillows and cushions into the widening gap around the keel that slowed the leak and allowed them to motor about ten miles to Puerto Plata. The fax from Hamburg indicated that the owner and his son having managed to partially plug the leak and were now at anchor in Puerto Plata. The owner who had taught nautical studies at the University of Heidelberg and his son were extremely knowledgeable and their efforts had clearly saved the yacht from sinking. We arranged to have the boat dry-docked at a small shipyard in Puerto Plata and found that in the rough seas they had encountered that the keel had almost completely separated from the hull. During the dry-dock inspection I found that the keel separation from the hull was due to sub-standard and inadequate repairs which had been undertaken to fix the boat following a storm that had impacted south Florida the year before. During the pre-purchase survey undertaken by a marine surveyor instructed by the professor when he bought the boat, the surveyor failed to closely inspect the laminates that formed the bond between the keel and the hull. Had he done a little homework the surveyor would have found that as a result of major structural damages sustained, this particular 42' Irwin had been declared a constructive total loss by her previous insurers. The damages sustained in the partial sinking off the Dominican coast as a result of the failure of the keel/hull laminates was unquestionably a latent, or hidden defect which would have been addressed under the *Inchmaree Clause*. The costs to repair the keel/hull join would have been excluded, but the other damages sustained would have been covered under the Policy. The claim was valid and should have been promptly settled under the terms and conditions of his Policy.

In the subrogation of his rights to insurers the professor and his underwriters would then have been entitled to sue the marine surveyor and the previous owner in the Southern District of Florida to recover their joint losses. As the repairs couldn't be undertaken in Puerto Plata I arranged a $5,000 tow to Puerto Rico and for the vessel to be hauled at Marina Puerto Del Rey, but not before calling Hamburg to advise the circumstances of the partial sinking. I confirmed that under the Inchmaree Clause the claim was a covered loss adding that the professor had agreed and would advance all the necessary expenses that could be reimbursed by underwriters at a later date. It was a Friday at 4:30PM in Germany when I reached Birgit in the claims department in Hamburg. She said that she was glad I had responded so quickly and had been able to assist the assured, who spoke no Spanish. Birgit told me that my proposal and the agreement with the Professor was acceptable and to proceed. I returned to Puerto Rico to confirm the dry-docking arrangements with Marina Puerto Del Rey and to confirm the tow. On Monday morning I received a call from the weasel who had returned to Hamburg for the week. Like a castrated pig screaming over the phone the *weasel* said that neither Birgit nor I had the right to make any arrangements to help or assist the Professor without his personal approval. The *weasel* said that even though it was probably a covered loss he was going to deny the claim believing that the Professor would not go to the expense of a lawsuit and simply pay everything out of his own pocket which is exactly what happened. Unethical, you bet, but a practice these brokers in Hamburg frequently engage in. The next day I decided to stop accepting assignments from these brokers in Hamburg. They now appoint fellow weasels to deal with their claims and losses in the Caribbean. This particular nefarious and reprehensible Hamburg weasel is unusual as German brokers and German insurance companies as a whole are generally honest, diligent and responsible. Now let's look at some technical stuff. There are a number of *clauses* and *warranties* that attach to an insurance policy and all are important. To provide equal fairness and to protect the assureds and the insurers for which they are acting, marine insurance adjusters must know and be conversant with the precise terms and conditions of the various marine policies issued by the players in the worldwide marine market. One example of clauses and warranties is the Inchmaree Clause sometimes referred to as the Negligence or Additional Perils Clause which attaches to marine hull policies.

The Inchmaree or Additional Perils Clause

1888 was a good year…for wine and insurance

The Inchmaree came about in 1888 as a result of the damages suffered by the steamer *Inchmaree*. Knowledge of the specific wording of the Inchmaree Clause is vitally important to anyone who deals in marine insurance, claims and losses. A good example of the interpretation of the Inchmaree would be a motor yacht that has a strut break due to defective casting; the shaft pulls out and both the shaft and propeller are lost. The owner of the vessel will be reimbursed the replacement cost of the propeller and the propeller shaft, but not the cost of the replacement strut. While slightly different from the claim of the German professor the Inchmaree Clause clearly would apply to both losses.

<u>The INCHMAREE Clause—Additional Perils</u>

"Subject to the conditions of this Policy, this insurance also covers loss of or damage to the Vessel directly caused by the following:

Accidents in going on or off, or while on dry-docks, graving docks, ways, gridirons or pontoons; Explosions on shipboard or elsewhere;

breakdown of motor generators or other electrical machinery and electrical connections thereto, bursting of boilers, breakage of shafts, or any latent defect in the machinery or hull (excluding the cost and expense of replacing or repairing the defective part)

Breakdown of or accidents to nuclear installations or reactors not on board the insured vessel; Contact with aircraft, rockets or similar missiles, or with any land conveyance; Negligence of Charterers and/or Repairers, provided such Charters and/or Repairers are not an Assured hereunder; Negligence of Masters, Officers, Crew or Pilots; provided such loss or damage has not resulted from the want of due diligence by the Assured, the Owners or Managers of the vessel, or any of them. Masters, Officers and Crew or Pilots are not to be considered Owners within the meaning of this clause should they hold shares in the vessel."

To the trained adjuster the interpretation of the Inchmaree is quite straightforward and if necessary must be carefully addressed in any report of a loss and detailed not only to the assured, but also to the underwriter's in-house claims handlers. Now you may rightly ask what the damages to a boiler on a 2,000 ton steam ship may have in relation to a propeller that was lost when a shaft broke on a 46' Bertram sport fisherman or the loss of an engine on a 50' Beneteau. The relationship is drawn not to the size of the vessel or the individual component, but to why and how the loss or damage was incurred. As mentioned earlier the Inchmaree clause takes its name from the 2,000 ton steamer whose boiler was damaged beyond repair; when attempting to charge the boilers, the pump failed when it was operated against a check valve which did not properly allow the water to flow from the pump to the boiler. It was never determined if the improper flow was because the engineer had improperly closed the valve or because it had been clogged by debris. The investigation did however clearly establish that the damages incurred were not the result of wear and tear. In an earlier case a steamer named *The Investigator* was wrecked by the explosion of her boiler under normal pressure. Even though the explosion was found to be due to negligent maintenance and operation by the ships engineers the Court of Appeal held that the assured could recover against his insurers, but for different reasons. Brett L.J. decided on the basis that the explosion by steam was *ejusdem generic* with fire. In the words of us commoners this simply means of the same kind of class (ejusdem generic or the same) Steam is related to and a result of fire.

Lord Selbourne L.C. was a bit more copious in his summation:

> "What the winds are to a sailing vessel, steam is to a steamer; and it is reasonable that marine insurers should bear the risks incident to a navigation by that kind of power, whether from excess of pressure in the boiler or from defects of safety valves, or from neglect or mismanagement making that dangerous which otherwise would not be so, as that they should bear losses occasioned by excessive pressure of winds and defects or mismanagement of a ships sails or tackle."

Being a persistent lot and not being pleased with a favorable ruling for the assured in the Court of Appeals even though the amount involved was only £72, the underwriters took the case to the House of Lords. The Investigator case was overruled. Their Lordships declined to treat the explosion of a boiler as a "peril of the sea" or a like peril, they reflected in their ruling that this was a type of accident that was as likely to occur ashore as well as at sea. While they had unquestionably achieved a victory in the House of Lords in 1888 underwriters introduced a clause known paradoxically as the Inchmaree clause emanating from a case that had held there was no such cover. The original 1888 Clause was a good start in clarification of coverage and over the years has been improved upon to such a degree that it impacts not only commercial but recreational vessels as well. The original wording of the 1888 Clause reads:

> "This insurance also specially to cover loss of, or damage to hull or machinery through the negligence of Master, Mariners, Engineers or Pilots, or through explosions, bursting of boilers, breakage of shafts, or through any latent defect in the machinery or hull, provided such loss or damage has not resulted from want of due diligence by the Owners of the vessel, or any of them, or by the manager."

The current Inchmaree clause has been refined and expanded over its 1888 ancestor and provides greater coverage which is required in the 21st Century. The changes between 1888 and 2004 are displayed bold type.

Accidents in going on or off, or while on dry-docks, graving docks, ways, gridirons or pontoons; Explosions on shipboard or elsewhere;

Breakdown of motor generators or other electrical machinery and electrical connections thereto, bursting of boilers, breakage of shafts, or any latent defect in the machinery or hull **(excluding the cost and expense of replacing or repairing the defective part)**

Breakdown of or accidents to nuclear installations or reactors not on board the insured vessel; Contact with aircraft, rockets or similar missiles, or with any land conveyance; Negligence of Charterers and/or Repairers, provided such Charters and/or Repairers are not an Assured hereunder; Negligence of Masters, Officers, Crew or Pilots; provided such loss or damage has not resulted from the want of due diligence by the Assured, **the Owners or Managers of the vessel, or any of them. Masters, Officers and Crew or Pilots are not to be considered Owners within the meaning of this clause should they hold shares in the vessel."**

While the Clause may expand the coverage and give you peace of mind if your local nuclear reactor has a melt down or if you come into contact with an aircraft, rocket or missile or get hit by a Greyhound Bus as you pass under the Chesapeake Bay Bridge it still will not repair or replace any defective or worn part that may have given rise to a claim. Let's go back to our 46' Bertram sport fisherman that lost its propeller when one of the shafts broke and the Perkins engine that disintegrated on the 50' Beneteau when the oil pump failed. The Bertram was at sea between St. Thomas, U.S. Virgin Islands and Sint Maarten in the Netherlands Antilles. About 40 NM from Sint Maarten the port engine started to run-away with RPMs that increased from 2300 to 5000 at which time the Bertram made an immediate swing to port. The owner moved the throttles to idle speed and checked the engine room. Everything appeared normal and both shafts were in place, at least as seen from inside the engine room.

The owner shut the engines down and the crewman went over the side to find that the port propeller shaft had broken at the cutlass bearing; the shaft end and the propeller had disappeared in a water depth that would prevent recovery. The owner returned to St. Thomas on one engine where the vessel was hauled. In the claim that was subsequently filed we pulled the remaining portion of the port shaft, the inspection revealed that the shaft had broken just aft of the cutlass bearing and the end piece of the shaft and propeller had simply dropped off. The rudder blade, rudder shaft and the strut displayed no impact damage indicating that when the shaft separated, the propeller and six inches of the aft portion of the shaft had not hit anything as it departed on its trip to the bottom. Metallurgical testing of the propeller shaft found that the failure was due to a latent defect in the stainless steel shaft material. Applying the principles of the Inchmaree, the dry-docking of the vessel, anti-fouling of the bottom (it had only been hauled two weeks before), lay-days while we awaited the new shaft and propeller and the $2,500.00 cost of the replacement propeller was considered part of the claim. The propeller shaft had failed due to a latent defect and therefore its $1,200.00 cost was not considered for underwriters account. While not an issue in the loss I suggested that the assured pull the starboard propeller shaft and have it inspected to insure that it was free of defect. In the case of the 50' Beneteau the engine had overheated as a result of loosing main lube oil pressure causing major internal component damage in the process. After receiving the claim we had the engine removed from the vessel and disassembled for inspection in the shop of an authorized Perkins dealer. The bench inspection revealed that the oil line to the lube oil pump had failed after which no oil was pumped from the crankcase. A close inspection of the copper oil line revealed that the failure was due to a latent/material defect and not due to wear and tear. It is possible that when the engine was manufactured the copper line may have been bent or structurally challenged during installation. Because of the location of the oil line inside the crankcase there would be no reasonable way a prudent assured could have inspected or known of the defective part prior to its failure. The claim was clearly a covered loss. Had the failure occurred on a newer or more expensive $200,000 or $300,000 engine, it may have been worthy of consideration for underwriters to evaluate the possibility of subrogation against the manufacturers for damages.

Subrogation on a $15,000 engine claim due to a defective fuel line, if it could be proven, may be considered by underwriters however, the cost of potential litigation simply would not be commercially viable. In any case the underwriters would clearly be responsible for repairing the engine, but may spend $30,000 in legal fees in an effort to recover $15,000 from the manufacturers and then lose the case. In many cases underwriters are committed to repair damaged engines where the required parts are addressed either new for old or through depreciation. There are cases where the assured may feel that he doesn't want to repair the engine as the cost of a new engine would be almost the same. No problem. The adjusted cost of the replacement parts would simply be applied against the cost of the new parts; the assured just pays the difference. This can be beneficial both to the assured who gets a brand new engine while the underwriters may save a bundle on the labor costs. In the case of the Beneteau the assured opted to have the damaged engine rebuilt at a cost of $8,000. The fair and reasonable labor costs were covered in full. The cost of the replacement parts were subject to a depreciation of 7% per annum and as the engine was five years old 35% of the parts costs were deemed the responsibility of the assured. The $10.00 cost of the fuel line, as a defective part (latent defect) was not included in the final settlement of the claim after the deductible had been applied. In these and many other claims that may involve the issue of latent defects the Inchmaree plays an important role in the adjustment and ultimate settlement of the loss. A full, thorough and proper investigation is extremely important to determine the *causa proxima* or proximate cause of the loss and every step in the process should include the participation of the assured. Expedient, fair and reasonable handling of claims by those in the field is probably the best marketing tool that brokers and underwriters have for selling new insurance policies. Most assureds don't read their insurance policies until they have a claim; others don't understand what coverage they have or how any claim is handled or adjusted. Some marine policies may have a provision stating new-for-old, others may be the reasonable cost of repairs or an annual depreciation for the replacement of damaged parts, it really depends on what coverage they bought or what they were sold by the producing broker. Many assureds believe that if they have an insurance policy on their boat/yacht they are covered for any loss that may occur. Unfortunately this isn't the case.

Many marine insurance policies, especially those on vessels are "named perils" policies whereas the assured has the burden of showing that both the loss and the peril which caused it fall within the meaning of the policy terms. *(Northwestern Mutual Life Insurance Co. v. Linard 1974 AMC 877)* However, this is not the case with "all risks" policies where the assured is only required to make a prima facia case that a loss has in fact occurred. The burden of proof then shifts to the insurer to show that the loss resulted from a cause excluded by the language of the policy *(Goodman V. Fireman's Fund Insurance Co., 1978 AMC 846)* now if this may sound a bit confusing you are not alone. The courts have often criticized the parties to a marine insurance contract for not making the policy or their intentions clear; therefore great care should be taken in purchasing an insurance policy and agreeing to the coverage conditions. Many assureds simply look for the lowest premium when they should first evaluate the security behind the policy and exactly what coverage is provided. When a claim occurs it's usually only at this time that the assured reads his policy and then becomes annoyed when he finds what is actually covered and what's not. Now that we've looked at the basics in the settlement of damages with marine claims let's take a look at what happens if the boat is lost in 10,000 feet of water, burns to the waterline or maybe is destroyed when the assured drives it over what he or she believes was an uncharted reef. About the time that the Queens of England began losing their heads there was an Elizabethan statute of 1601 that pretty well described that the main object of marine insurance was to protect the individual person or corporation against a catastrophic loss. "By means of a Policy of Insurance it cometh to pass that upon the loss or perishing of any ship ther followeth not the undoing of any man but the loss lighteth rather easily upon many than heavily upon few." In todays less poetic terms this simply means spread the risk; which is why in the London Market you may find a number of underwriters on the risk. Total Loss, Actual Total Loss or Constructive Total Loss? A total loss may be either an actual total loss or a constructive total loss and unless a different intention appears from the terms of the policy, insurance against total loss includes a constructive as well as an actual total loss. No doubt this was written by a lawyer to make legal interpretation a requirement!

In simpler terms when addressing the issue of a total loss which also may be applied to a CTL (Constructive Total Loss) the definition provided in the Marine Insurance Act states:

> "Where the subject-matter insured is destroyed, or so damaged as to cease to be a thing of the kind insured, or where the assured is irretrievably deprived thereof, there is an actual total loss."(Section 57)

The definition and requirements of a constructive total loss in England are more precise than those in the United States, but generally say the same thing.

> "Subject to any express provision in the policy there is a constructive total loss where a subject-matter insured is reasonably abandoned on account of its actual total loss appearing to be unavoidable, or because it could not be preserved from actual total loss without an expenditure which would exceed its value when the expenditure had been incurred."

There is a constructive total loss when through a covered loss the assured is deprived of his vessel, or the cost of salvage or recovery would exceed the value of the ship, or the cost of repairing the damages would exceed the value of the vessel following repairs. Let's say a two year old $100,000 yacht sinks in 10,000 feet of water; clearly salvers can't recover the yacht at this depth. The yacht is declared a total loss. Another ten year old $100,000 yacht sinks in 100 feet of water 40 NM off Cabo Gracious de Dio on the Caribbean coast of Honduras; the closest commercial salvers are in Panama who provide an estimate of $70,000 to refloat the yacht plus another $7,500 for the tow of the wreck to the dry-dock in Colon, Panama. With known expenses of $77,500 in addition to the costs of dry-docking, repair and restoration of a yacht that has been submerged, which may exceed $40,000, underwriters declared the vessel a CTL or construc-tive total loss. In the case of the *Armar* (1954 AMC 1674) the court held: "In the calculation of repair and recovery costs it is proper to include expenditure necessary to deliver the ship from its peril to a port of safety and thereafter to make it a seaworthy vessel. Accordingly, in addition to repair costs, the expenses of salvage dry-dock and surveys, pilotage and towage and superintendence are allowable." This brings us to the subject of under-or-over insuring a yacht. If it's underinsured say for $75,000 when its true value is $150,000 the assured may save a few dollars on the premium.

However, if the yacht incurs major damages that represent 85% or more of the insured value (and this percentage varies from insurer to insurer depending on their claims procedures) the underwriter can right-fully avoid the hassle and heartburn of battling with an assured during the repair process, declare the vessel a CTL, pay the agreed value of $75,000 and then sell the wreck for whatever they can get for it. If it's really a $150,000 yacht the assured looses big time and there's absolutely nothing he or she can do about it. In the case of valuation concerning commercial vessels the *Contributory Value of a Ship* is addressed under Rule XVII of the York/Antwerp Rules which stipulate that contribution to general aver-age (the ratable contribution towards the cost of repairs) is to be made on the actual net values of the property at the termination of the adventure (the time of the incident). In the United States it is common practice to base the vessel's contributory value on the sale prices of similar vessels which have been sold by their owners within a recent period. In the case of yachts it's a different ball game. In one particular case I found that the assured had obtained an abandoned and derelict twenty-five year old 45' sailing yacht for $35,000 in cash and a beat up, 20 year old Ford station wagon. To obtain insurance he needed a survey which was obtained from an obliging surveyor who, after having been told by the new owner what equipment was on board and after having a couple of beers in the cockpit, produced an official looking Report of Survey that reflected a value of $90,000. Had the surveyor taken the time to inspect the boat to determine its true condition to see if the engine and generator were running (they weren't), verify the purchase price paid by his client or even confirm the values of comparables and then submitted an accurate report, the underwriter would not have accepted this unacceptable risk. Sixty days after inception of the policy the vessel sank at its mooring in 30' of water. Using SCUBA gear I dove on the vessel and found that water had entered the hull through the propeller shaft log. As the engine and transmission were little more than hunks of rusted metal the propeller shaft had been removed and the opening sealed with a wood plug. The plug worked loose and dropped off. In spite of the flawed survey the underwriter had accepted the risk and was stuck with the claim. To salvage the vessel another plug was inserted to seal the propeller shaft and the vessel was pumped, refloated and cleaned with fresh water at a cost of $2,000. The VHF-FM radio and depth sounder were replaced based on an adjustment of 80% (the value was reduced by 20% per year—but not less than 20% of the actual replacement costs).

The assured did not anticipate the vessel being repaired and was banking on receiving $90,000. Because of the age of the vessel, the applicable 80% depreciation of the parts and a deductible of $1,000 the assured ultimately received a net settlement of $10,200. After the claim was settled the policy was promptly canceled. The underwriter had a strong case against the assured and the surveyor based on their material misrepresentations; these material misrepresentations included the value of the yacht, the unseaworthiness of the vessel, which could have voided the Policy from inception. However, if a Declaratory Action had been filed in denial of the claim, considering a hull value of $90,000, the assured would have undoubtedly found a lawyer to take the case on a contingency. To defend such a spurious action would immediately require underwriters instructing counsel at an initial cost of not less than $10,000 thereby opening the door to lengthy and expensive litigation. On the other hand in not denying the claim and dealing with the loss in accordance with the terms and conditions of the policy underwriters exposure was limited to $10,200. Another similar case of over insurance involved a ten year old 50' Beneteau that had been retired from charter service and changed ownership twice in the last five years. The new owner purchased the Beneteau for $125,000. He insured the yacht for $225,000 with an insurer who didn't require a survey and failed to ask the purchase price paid when he bought the vessel. A year passed without incident, then on a passage from Curacao in the Dutch West Indies to Panama the vessel had engine problems near Cartagena, Colombia. While passing through the area known as the Bancos de Salmedina, the vessel struck a reef, was badly holed and partially sank. The assured temporarily plugged the hole in the port hull, pumped out as much water as possible and called for assistance. The Beneteau was refloated and towed into Cartagena for US$5,000, followed by a dry-docking at a local shipyard. The damages were not simply limited to the hull, keel and the rudder which had broken off, the vessel had also sustained major damage to the interior joinery and sea water had penetrated all the electrical wiring which had shorted all the electronics. In speaking with the shipyard and local repair contractors I determined that the vessel could be repaired for a bit under US$100,000, but the repairs could take up to six months. The assured was quite upset with my findings, didn't want the vessel repaired and insisted the yacht to be declared a CTL demanding a payment of the salvage fees plus $225,000.00. When I declined to render the vessel a CTL because of her insured value, the assured decided that maybe we should talk.

In our discussions we went over each individual item that had been damaged comparing it to the repair estimates, adding those items that needed to be obtained from suppliers in Florida, shipping and customs brokers charges and subtracting those items that were clearly betterment's. The vessel was equipped with 48NM (nautical mile) radar, but the owner said if it was to be replaced he would only accept an upgraded 72 NM radar. I agreed adding that the difference in price between the two would be for his account. The same formula was applied to the wind generator, sailing instruments and the GPS. The hull had been penetrated when it came into contact with the reef resulting in a three x five foot hole at the waterline on the port side. The joinery in the main saloon, including the settee frame and cushions had been torn away as a result of the flooding of the interior. At least three feet of water had entered the hull flooding the two forward cabins and two aft cabins. The navigation area just aft of amidships to starboard had a white salt film covering all of the instruments. When electrical wiring, starters, alternators in fact anything electrical is subjected to salt water flooding or penetration my experience dictates that it must be renewed. While you may temporarily dip and clean starters and alternators in an alcohol bath and dry them they should be replaced, if not these components will ultimately fail, and probably at the worst possible time. Salt water will migrate through the PVC sheathing protecting electrical wires. If a vessel's electrical wires have been submerged in salt water I believe the wiring should always be renewed. To not do so may save a little money now, but could give rise to a major fire claim later. The hull had been damaged over an area of about fifteen square feet however in restoring the original Gel Coat the repaired area may actually extend to twenty square feet. When we together reviewed the hull repair and the estimate to refinish the Gel Coat the assured became adamant that he wanted the entire hull refinished in Awl Grip. I agreed this would be quite acceptable and definitely improve the appearance of the original faded dark blue Gel Coat however, I pointed out that underwriters would only be responsible for the cost of repairs limited to the twenty square foot of damaged area; the assured would be responsible for the balance. When the color had returned to his face I read him the conditions in the policy that clearly stated that repairs and refinishing of the hull was limited only to the damaged areas.

The assured then offered the suggestion that his underwriters ship the yacht to Miami or Fort Lauderdale where the repairs could be completed. I agreed that this would be an excellent idea, but the costs would not be at underwriter's expense. He asked why? Clearly it was now time to explain the facts of marine insurance and the coverage afforded under his Policy. I began by pointing out that most blue water or offshore marine policies are generally ones of indemnification and his was no exception. If an assured has a loss that gives rise to a claim he must always, as soon as possible, report the loss to the producing insurance broker or the underwriter direct and must then act as a prudent uninsured. He didn't quite understand the assured *acting as a prudent uninsured* so I explained. Assume you had no insurance and suffered a loss, what would you do to protect your yacht, personal effects or other property on board? You would naturally do whatever is necessary to protect and mitigate your damages and as best as you can insure that no further damages are incurred. The assured may also submit receipts for reimbursement of the reasonable expenses he or she may have incurred in protecting the yacht. Most policies include a provision often referred to as the sue and labor clause that states, "Reasonable expenses incurred by you in attempting to avert or minimize a loss covered by the insuring agreement will be paid by us (the insurer) whether successful or not. These will be paid in addition to the sum insured under the specific sections without application of the insuring agreement deductible, but a coinsurance provision applies whereby we (the insurers) will pay 80% and you (the assured) will pay 20% of such expenses. The percentages are subject to agreement but generally are 80% for the insurers and 20% for the account of the assureds. If an assured does not take the necessary steps to protect his yacht underwriters could deny any reimbursement of these extraordinary damages or the claim itself. The assured then said that in addition to the damages sustained when he struck the reef a few days after the yacht had been taken to the shipyard, his Zodiac dinghy and 35 HP Mercury engine had been stolen, he had left the dinghy on the dock without locking them. The theft of the dinghy and outboard was therefore a separate occurrence, covered under the policy but subject to the deductible of the tender coverage. Applied psychology: unless the initial gut feeling is that you are dealing with a fraudster and a fraudulent claim I feel it's very important to display a genuine empathy towards the assured and have compassion in dealing with his or her dilemma. Alternatively, consume a reasonable quantity of club soda to settle the gut feeling brought on by a fraudster.

I went on to explain that as his yacht was insured for $225,000 and the cost of repairs would be less than $100,000 this is the amount that underwriters would be responsible for once they accepted the claim. The adjuster has no responsibility or authority to accept or deny any claim which is the sole prerogative of the insurers. The assured then admitted that even though the Beneteau had been purchased for $125,000 he had increased the insurance coverage by $100,000 because he believed that if he somehow lost the boat he would be able to buy a newer and even better boat. Big Mistake! As there were qualified repairers in Cartagena that could carry out professional repairs and restore the boat, even if the assured didn't wish to have the boat repaired in Cartegena the policy had no provisions to pay for shipping of the yacht back to the United States. The assured clearly believed that because of the extent of the damages to his yacht he would be receiving a check for the value of his yacht. Had he insured the vessel for its true value of $125,000 he would have had received this amount in full settlement of his claim. Unfortunately he got greedy and believed he could show a handsome profit if the Beneteau was lost. As marine insurance is one of indemnification the assured would have been tasked with advancing the repairs costs, submitting the paid receipts for approval and reimbursement. While not required to do so, in most cases as a gesture of good faith and in hopefully reaching a prompt and amicable agreement with the assured on the nature and extent of the damages, underwriters will generally advance at least part if not all of the fair and reasonable repair costs in an effort to assist the assureds. After contacting the underwriter by telephone I was authorized on behalf of the insurers to reimburse the US$5,000 in salvage charges and to offer the assured without prejudice US$95,000 (which was the actual cost of repairs) in full and final settlement of his claim. Underwriters even went as far as to waive the US$4,500 deductible. It took six weeks for the assured to ponder his limited options. He subsequently accepted underwriters offer of settlement and sold the Beneteau to a Canadian do-it-yourselfer for US$4,500. Two years later when I was in Cartagena I was told that the Beneteau was being used as a houseboat. Had it not been for a bit of greed the Beneteau could either have been repaired and restored or been declared a CTL providing for a full recovery of the $125,000 purchase price. In any case the assured should consider himself lucky that he received at least $99,500 of his $125,000 investment.

My experience with insurance brokers is that while there are a few who don't, most insurance brokers deal promptly and efficiently when they receive a Notice of Loss. During the time when I was actively dealing with claims for an insurance underwriting agent in the north of England who was acting for various European insurers I had the pleasure of working with Ms. Olga Portocarrero of the offices of Jorge Rivera Insurance in San Juan, Puerto Rico. Mr. Jorge Rivera is knowledgeable and professional in all matters of insurance and Olga, while not necessarily an expert in marine claims, never hesitated to call me nights or weekends if she needed specific help in the interpretation of a policy or to report a loss while the paper work was being shuffled. Promptly responding to a claim saves time and money for both the assureds and their underwriters. As surveyors and adjusters we have a solemn responsibility without prejudice, to fairly and accurately investigate and evaluate all claims and if necessary report the fair and reasonable cost of repairs in accordance with the terms and conditions agreed in the policy. If an assured disputes the findings of a qualified adjuster they have every right, at their expense to appoint their own expert to make their own determination. Insurance is meant to protect and provide assureds a means of recovery in the event of a fortuitous loss, it is not intended to provide a profit.

The Market and American Lawyers

The Challenges....

UK and European insurers who continue to use insurance applications that are limited to a dozen or so of irrelevant questions, not requesting a current survey or accepting condition and valuation surveys from unqualified surveyors are doomed to failure and have become a cash cow to US attorneys. Over lunch at the former Marine Club in London, a tennis court away from the Lloyd's building (old and new) the moaning and sobbing of underwriters decrying the aggressiveness of US admiralty attorneys and condemnation of the *bloody* injustice of the American legal system was frequently a lunch time topic. While indeed there are aggressive attorneys on both sides of the Atlantic the affected underwriters need to first look at their own failings that allow these lawyers to prevail. In years past the stalwarts of the marine market such as Robin Kershaw, Roger Fitter and a host of others who, while not always generally were able to avoid the spurious litigation that prevails in today's market. However, even these good guys of Lime Street were occasionally overshadowed by the mischievous behavior of others who occupied an adjacent *Box*. One particular marine underwriter after being accused of defrauding his own syndicate quickly departed London and is said to have opened a toy store in Tampa, Florida.

The co-owner of the toy store was a lady friend from the Virgin Islands who previously had the *pen* to bind his dubious policies. In the process of denying his claims the same underwriter insisted that all those who filed claims submit to a polygraph tests. In my private and professional life I have had the pleasure or sometimes displeasure to meet a gaggle of prime ministers, a number of scurrilous criminals, famous and infamous business people and few eminent producers, actors and writers, to many to list and besides it may sound like bragging, which I detest on a par with stupidity. However, as a whole I've been very fortunate to have met some truly nice and honest people. I believe that everyone you meet or may have dealings with will or should, make an impression and have a positive influence on your life. It's up to you to determine the good from the evil and direct your life accordingly. I would not wish to give you the impression that it was easy to say no to sizable under-the-table payments offered to alter claim reports or approve inflated salvage contracts because it wasn't. As a result I didn't become wealthy,

I also had a son who instead of attending a university at a reduced tuition rate as a resident of Puerto Rico wanted to attend a college in Chestertown, Maryland while at the same time I was also working to complete my masters' degree. Illicit payments would have gone a long way in keeping up with both of our tuition fees, books and all the other gear that two guys need to complete an education, but the ultimate price was simply too high. Had I accepted the illegitimate bribes offered by salvage companies or the kick-backs offered to approve inflated repair bills regularly paid by boat yards to the less than honorable surveyors and adjusters I'd undeniably be just as evil. While the do-gooders frequently speak of rehabilitation, I believe that once a hooker—always a hooker. Having refused to accept these illicit payments, my financial status may be wanting, but it allows me to sleep well at night with a clear conscience. I've purposely pointed an accusing finger at a number of assureds as a source of the fraud emanating from claims, but that's not the whole story. While there are a number of educated, skilled and experienced underwriters, agents, brokers and I would include claims managers and their respective staffs in the equation, there is an equal or maybe greater number who don't have a clue about marine insurance policies, coverage issues or the requirements and procedures in fairly dealing with claims. And then there are those weasels in positions of influence that are well placed in the insurance fraud chain who will steal from you even before you might have a claim. Eliot Spitzer, the New York Attorney General recently filed a complaint against Marsh & McLennan implicating AIG and Ace alleging they rigged phony bids and accepted millions in illegal payments for steering business to preferred insurers. The criminal charges suggest that Spitzer considers 'contingent commissions' a criminal act. Two AIG managers and one assistant vice president from Ace have already pleaded guilty to charges related to the probe. Claims industry expert, Mr. Stephen Hartigan, director of JTW Reinsurance Consultants of the UK recently told the *Lloyd's List*, "London's global status has taken a pasting for too long. The market's lack of efficient, speedy and robust claims handling and settlement processing has left it wide open to international criticism and damaged its reputation." Mr. Hartigan, as an English gentleman, didn't mention that the lack of speedy, efficient and robust claims handling is also why the London market has paid through the nose for legal representation and high jury awards. It is an unfortunate fact that some of these self anointed insurance experts are not experts at all, but in many cases are just outright swindlers. One of these swindlers was the claims manager of one of the largest marine insurance brokers in Fort Lauderdale, Florida, as side-line he also covertly owned a marine salvage business. The surveyors and loss adjusters he put on his payroll for obvious reasons were sworn to secrecy. In return for a percentage of the illegal gains *his* surveyors and adjusters were paid to direct all the damaged boats (constructive total losses) to his salvage company for a reduced and predetermined salvage value that he would personally determine.

During the years he was in control of claims the underwriters lost hundreds of thousands of dollars, never catching on until a disgruntled ex-employee exposed the scam causing him to be quietly fired by his employer. Most owners of small boats and yachts in purchasing insurance believe that having insurance means everything is insured. Unfortunately this isn't the case. There are a myriad of policies available which are currently being offered to the boating community, all are different in the coverage they provide, adjustments, deductibles, some apply depreciation, others don't and other seemingly insignificant little things called warranties and conditions which cover such things as named operators and navigational limits. These warranties and conditions which are not insignificant items include where you can use your boat (navigational limits), who can drive your boat, (named operators) and normally include the requirements of a current survey. Responsible underwriters are now making efforts to insure that their assureds know what the policies cover and through responsible brokers asking that assureds read their policies when they are first issued. Early on in my career I was very fortunate to have met and befriended Barrie Harding. Barrie, an Englishman with a brilliant flair for designing and the implementation of innovative marine insurance programs has probably forgotten more about marine insurance than most agents, producers, underwriters or claims people will ever learn during their careers. In addition to being knowledgeable he was a focused family man, outstanding administrator and creative. While the executive director of a leading London insurance broker he designed and implemented a yacht program for Hull & Company in Fort Lauderdale that would soon make them one of the leading marine insurance producers in the United States. Richard (Dick) Hull was a hard working and imaginative entrepreneur who in recognizing his skills, eventually hired Barrie elevating him to the position of Deputy Managing Director of their operations in London. Barrie skillfully guided Hull & Company of both the United Kingdom and the United States to even greater heights of recognition and profitability. His accomplishments did not go unnoticed by the competition in spite of the questionable competence of Hull & Company's UK managing director who lived in Tampa and a crony of Dick Hull. Only a short time after its formation Hull & Company's London operation and Barrie Harding were both shall we say, liquidated. In quest of new horizons Barrie subsequently got caught up with some individuals who, unbeknownst to him at the time were involved in some rather vague business activities in

Brussels and the Principality of Monaco. After becoming aware that all was not well, Barrie promptly extracted himself and moved on.

The classic end to this saga was that the Monaco operation was soon dissolved and Hull & Company of Fort Lauderdale is no longer the force it once was in the marine market in the United States. A few words about yacht brokers: A number of those who are buying a Yacht for the first time, a yacht being something over 25', has a bed and a toilet (so as not to offend the nautical aficionados *berth* and *head*), and who may need professional help in the purchase generally turn to a yacht broker. Over the last 30 years I've been exposed to enough yacht brokers to fill the Queen Mary and would caution both buyers and sellers of any boat to exercise extreme care when a yacht broker surfaces. On a few occasions during condition and valuation surveys certain brokers have asked that I overlook specific cosmetic and other deficiencies while others have offered *under-the-table* bribes to increase values on yachts big and small. This doesn't mean that all yacht brokers are shall I say less than honorable, just a few. On the other hand when speaking privately to a number of buyers and sellers they tend to generally concur that most yacht brokers just need to be carefully monitored to insure they really are looking out for your interests, not just their commission. The best advice I recently heard was forthcoming from a recent buyer of a Hatteras 60', "don't give them any money or sign anything unless your attorney say's it is OK." As to the legal aspects if you may need an attorney who is reliable and has comprehension of both corporate and admiralty law; in New York call Lars Forsberg, Esq. of the firm of Holland & Knight. In South Carolina go to Dale Akins, Esq. of Novit, Scarminach & Akins or Gerald M. Finkel, Esq. of Finkel & Altman or Philip Gerson of Gerson & Schwartz in Miami all are in the phone book. Because they're good they're always busy—but worth the wait. Unfortunately the leader in the field, Myles Tralins was recently lost in a tragic automobile accident in England. In returning briefly to yacht brokers I must admit that over the years I have met two brokers who made a positive impression as being trustworthy, honest, knowledgeable, experienced and both believe in, and displayed integrity. Rex Martin in Lafayette, California (across from San Francisco) and Alan Stowell of Alan's Yacht Sales in Fort Lauderdale, Florida. Their yacht brokerage businesses are not the size of Allied Richard Bertram, Gilman or Fraser, but both are honest and work hard for their clients. Alan and Rex are not corporate minions and don't waste your time just to meet the sales projections and profit margins mandated by the *big guys*.

Utmost Good Faith

Uberrimae Fidei......

Insurance companies in the United States or in the case of Lloyd's syndicates or individual underwriters and their reinsurers are betting that after you pay your premium and set sail, you will abide by the agreed terms and conditions of the policy and will at all times exercise *uberrimae fidei*—utmost good faith. You on the other hand rely on your insurers to pay any fair and reasonable claim that may arise from a fortuitous loss, which in plain English simply means accidental. You won't be paid for wear and tear which simply means that if your 70' mast falls down because of a rusted stay or a corroded fitting that failed or your 2,000 horsepower MTU high performance diesel engines blew up because you hadn't followed the factory maintenance regime, your claim for damages most assuredly will be denied. If you have a lawyer (read *shyster*) that thinks they can file a lawsuit and pressure your insurers into 'negotiating' a settlement even though the policy clearly states there's no coverage, pay close attention to his proposal, he may be on to something. If the lawyer is willing to work on a contingency basis you have nothing to lose except maybe your self respect. Courts are not generally sympathetic to insurance companies and the insurance companies know it. To defend even a frivolous lawsuit can cost thousands of dollars, while it's bad for the underwriters it's an equal blessing for lawyers and the experts they employ. The lawyers for the underwriters must believe that they can win the case and that a *good* legal precedent can be established to deter spurious litigation in the future. If they have made it this far they then must convince the underwriters that litigating the case would be a positive move. If not, the underwriter will fold like a deck of cards and 'negotiate' a settlement with the shyster. I have personally been involved in cases where there is a clear breach of the contract of insurance, but in considering the cost of litigation and with no guarantee that the underwriters will prevail, they will try to negotiate and pay the claim. Beware though as there are still some insurance underwriters that in dealing with an inflated or fraudulent claim will spend what ever necessary to insure justice is done or attempt to establish a favorable legal precedent. If you may be feeling sorry for the poor insurance company or underwriter who is burdened with paying frivolous claims, don't, eventually they pass these costs on to you, me and everyone else who has insurance on his boat.

I was recently involved in a $300,000.00 claim where the loss was not the result of an insured peril and therefore no coverage existed; the vessel sank because of her rotten wood hull. The owner believed that an *All Risks* policy meant that his underwriters should pay and found a lawyer to take the case on a contingency. Before he filed the lawsuit I met with the owner and believe he would have happily accepted a negotiated settlement of $200,000.00 and walk away a happy-camper. There was clearly no cover under the Policy, but considering the case was scheduled for trial in Texas, a State known for its own interpretation of the law and its high jury awards a commercial decision should be made where a negotiated settlement is taken into consideration. Instead of attempting to negotiate a resolution the lawyers convinced the underwriter to litigate the case. Insurers ultimately spent $150,000.00 in attorneys' fees to defend the case and lost. While undoubtedly distasteful, a $200,000.00 settlement beats the hell out of a final bill of $450,000.00 plus interest. In another case the adjusted claim settlement was $900.00, the assured refused to accept the settlement and sued for $90,000.00 in damages. The lawyer for the insurers didn't answer the complaint or appear at a number of hearings so the judge rendered a Default Judgment. The insurers had to retain another lawyer to sue the first lawyer to make him pay the $90,000.00 the court had awarded to the plaintiffs. It was a messy affair that took three years to sort out. The bad thing is that in spite of a fraudulent claim to begin with the assured literally stole $90,000.00 and got away with it. This is *bad* legal precedent. In another case, (these by the way are all cases that were heard in a United States District Court, the British and European courts don't tolerate such nonsense) underwriters denied a $135,000.00 claim then spent almost as much to obtain a ruling in favor of the underwriters. Six months later the ruling was overturned on appeal because the lawyer acting for underwriters had failed to list his witness as an expert; the expert's opinion testimony was thrown out when he was deemed a lay-witness. Another *bad* legal precedent. Marine insurance and admiralty law in the United States and in the United Kingdom is based primarily on *precedents*, what's happened before and what case law has been applied. In the review of claims and losses over the years I've regularly used a number of reference books which are readily available especially now with Internet access. The field of insurance law is broad and far reaching and therefore it's really not practical to attempt to recite all the peculiar aspects on the subject and in any case I'm not licensed to practice law. There are however certain subjects that every marine loss adjuster or surveyor who renders an opinion concerning seaworthiness or the value of a yacht must be aware as these particular subjects that play a critical role in the evaluation of any vessel before or after a loss.

One example of how a marine surveyor based in St. John, USVI got his client in deep *you know what* was exposed when I was dealing with damages to a vessel following a hurricane. By chance I had seen this particular yacht a few years back when it fell in the shipyard at Virgin Gorda in the British Virgin Islands. Because the vessel was severely damaged the underwriters didn't repair the yacht but declared her a constructive total loss or CTL, paid the policyholder and sold the wreck for $100.00. The wreck was later sold to a new owner who had it surveyed so he could obtain new insurance, no problem so far. The marine surveyor in St. John traveled to Virgin Gorda conducted the survey, put a $150,000.00 value on the yacht but left out, didn't mention or omitted from the survey that the yacht had not been completely repaired and had been declared a constructive total loss the previous year. During my inspection for underwriters in relation to the hurricane claim I found failures in the hull laminates, bulkheads and a bent mast all which had occurred as a result of the fall in Virgin Gorda, not from the high winds of a hurricane. A further investigation found that only superficial repairs had been done to the hull and the mast and rigging had never been replaced, renewed or repaired. The surveyor in the U.S. Virgin Islands was either incompetent, crooked, or both. If he was incompetent he could have been sued by the new owner unless the new owner was part of the conspiracy to defraud the underwriters. The new owner said he had bought the boat from a guy who said he purchased the wreck for $100.000.00, of course neither could prove what they paid for the wrecked yacht, explaining that the transactions were in cash. A $100.00 wreck/CTL with minimal repairs, bent mast and delaminated hull that's sold two months later for $100,000.00—yeah right. If you believe that I've got a bridge in Brooklyn you may be interested in. Following a little research underwriters were able to be extracted from this mess unscathed, but what would have happened if the yacht had sunk in the Puerto Rican trench (the deepest water in the world and a common place for unexplained sinkings) they would have been faced with a $150,000.00 claim. Another interesting aspect to this is how stupid insurance underwriters can be when accepting survey reports of condition and valuation. The surveyor in St. John was a member of one of the US based surveyor organizations and is supposed to be qualified to inspect and report on a small yacht, the surveyor did not hold any qualifications in yacht valuation appraisal. In the next chapter I'll go into the need for marine surveyors and yacht appraisers to hold the required qualifications that would permit them to do the job that insurers and banks expect from their services.

Qualifications
Claims—Seaworthiness

Blind Eye Knowledge—What's Important?

The American Society of Appraisers in Washington is a multi-disciplined organization of accredited appraisers certified in various disciplines such as real estate, jewelry, fine art, aircraft and yachts and ships. Membership and accreditation requirements are rigid and necessarily so. The certifications are awarded based on education (a college degree is one of the requirements), experience (at least five years) and a rigid test that can take up to eight hours to complete. Once accreditation is obtained it is mandated that the person maintain it by qualified continuing education. Like most worthwhile professional qualifications it requires a laborious and time consuming effort to achieve. It has surprised me that few marine surveyors have sought or attained designation in the valuation field. As of January 1, 2004 there were only 11 accredited senior yacht appraisers in the United States, 14 certified in commercial vessels (one is from Argentina) and only 2 certified in both yachts and commercial vessels. As an accredited senior appraiser of yachts and ships in the Caribbean area I've often wondered why unqualified surveyors would perilously venture into the valuation field considering the frightening exposure of malpractice litigation and potential damages. During the discovery process an admiralty lawyer would quickly establish the lack of qualifications. In the case of the St. John surveyor's condition and valuation report the underwriter blindly accepted it and didn't question its contents. Now there's absolutely nothing wrong with a marine surveyor indicating in his report a value that's been copied out of one of the brokers' publications that put forth varying figures or even what the surveyor may personally perceive as a reasonable value, as long as the source is clearly identified. Insurers are well aware that these value books are generally inflated because the information is provided by yacht brokers for yacht brokers and are purely self serving. If the surveyor wants to indicate a value based on his best guess or from one of the price guides produced by the yacht brokers this should be stated in his report. It's then up to the underwriters to make the call as to whether the value stated is real or not. In the case of the St. John surveyor the underwriters in good faith had issued a $150,000 insurance policy on a yacht that had only recently been declared a constructive total loss and was sold for $100.00.

The underwriter was seriously mislead (material misrepresentation) by the assured and his surveyor. The underwriter had problems with the surveyor in the past yet still continued accepting his reports—a really dumb move. Had it not been for a little *local knowledge* the underwriters would have paid $150,000.00 in settlement of the claim and then next year jacked up the rates with you and I picking up the tab. On the other hand foolish and irresponsible underwriting has lead to a growing number of marine insurers who have seen their reinsurance disappear and forcing them to stop writing policies. Many of these buffoons simply dropped from sight because their underwriting procedures and guidelines had been so ridiculous. Do you think life insurance companies would stay in business if they issued policies to terminally ill individuals or accepted medical reports from unlicensed physicians—not likely. We live in a litigious society and based on the *deep pockets* principal insurers are regularly in the cross hairs. Insurance companies frequently discover they incur substantial losses based on inflated valuations submitted by marine surveyors who hold no qualifications or credentials as appraisers. As everyone in the marine industry knows, there are a number of surveyors who in spite of various initials of qualification behind their names have questionable levels of knowledge and skill. A few courageous insurers who have been embroiled in litigation as a result of surveyor's negligence have successfully sued these individuals and obtained judgments. But unless the surveyor has an E&O policy that will respond or possibly some sizable assets there's no purpose in engaging in foolish litigation. Even if you may secure a judgment and win a million bucks from Joe Surveyor of Fort Lauderdale, how do you collect damages awarded from someone who lives in a rented apartment in a seedy part of town, is behind in his car payments and has trouble meeting his child support or alimony payments. On the other hand it's surprising the number of professional and responsible marine surveyors who do not have errors and omissions insurance. While we're on the subject of legalities let's look at some of the important issues that I raised earlier which have an impact on the evaluation of claims.

NON-DISCLOSURE/MATERIAL MISREPRESENTATION

The provision of the Marine Insurance Act dealing with disclosure and representations are set forth in sections 18, 19 and 20 of the Act, which deserves to be set out in full. The *duty*, which is to disclose the facts known, to one party and not to the other, was explained by Lord Justice Fletcher Moulton in *Joel v. Law Union & Crown Insurance* (Joel v. Law Union & Crown Insurance [1908] 2 K.B. 863 at 884)

> "The duty is a duty to disclose, and you cannot disclose what you do not know. The obligation to disclose, therefore, necessarily depends on the knowledge you possess."

The duty is to disclose to the underwriters and a prospective assured who discloses matters to his agent or broker which the latter does not pass on to underwriters is nevertheless in breach of his duty. It is no defence for the assured even if the omission to disclose is innocent. Thus in *Bates v. Hewitt* Cockburn C.J. said:

"It is well established law that it is immaterial whether the omission to communicate a material fact arises from indifference or a mistake or from it not being present to the mind of the assured that the fact was one which it was material to make known."

The duty of disclosure under these sections continues up to the moment at which a binding contract is concluded, and returns into existence, for instance, at the time of renewal of the policy. Sections 18 of the Marine Insurance Act, read as follows:

"S.18 Disclosure by assured

1.   Subject to the provisions of this section, the assured must disclose to the insurer, before the contract is concluded, every material circumstance which is known to the assured, and the assured is deemed to know every circumstance which, in the ordinary course of business, ought to be known by him. If the assured fails to make such disclosure, the insurer may avoid the contract.

2.   Every circumstance is material which would influence the judgment of a prudent insurer in fixing the premium, or determining whether he will take the risk."

"The duty of disclosure, as defined or circumscribed by ss. 18 and 19, is one aspect of the overriding duty of utmost good faith, *uberrimae fidei,* mentioned in s.17. The actual insurer is thereby entitled to the disclosure to him of every fact which would influence the judgment of a prudent insurer in fixing the premium or determining he will take the risk."

BURDEN OF PROOF

If a vessel sinks in a calm sea the Burden of Proof shifts from the underwriters to the assured. The assured then has the sole responsibility to make out a prima facie case that the loss was proximately caused by an insured peril. The level of proof depends upon the circumstances of the loss. Where, for instance, the ship is lost with all hands and nothing more is known there may be a presumption of loss by perils of the sea. Not so where there are survivors and the circumstances of the loss are known. In response to a prima facie case underwriters may put up an alternative explanation of the loss falling outside the cover, or may put the assured to a strict burden of proof.

UNSEAWORTHINESS

The Fifth Circuit Court of Appeals required underwriters to prove affirmatively unseaworthiness as a cause of any sinking in order to defend successfully a suit under the American hull form of policy when the loss being claimed was caused by sinking *(Tropical Marine Prod. V. Birmingham Fire Ins. Co.,* 247 F2d 16). More recently the Fifth Circuit reiterated that a seaworthy boat's unexplained sinking was fortuitous and thus presumably caused by an insured peril of the sea *(Darien Bank v. The Travelers Indemnity.* 1985 AMC 1813).

These American decisions appear to endorse the English concept of entry of seawater per se being a peril of the sea. Yet in other cases involving unexplained sinkings, American courts have firmly stated:

> Where a ship sinks in fair weather and calm seas, it is presumed that the loss was due to unseaworthiness.
>
> —*(Federazione Italiana Dei Corsozi Agrari v. Mandas, Compania de Vapores, S.A.,* 1968 AMC 315).

> The vessel having sunk for reasons and causes unknown, its unseaworthiness is presumed.
>
> —*(Martin & Robertson v. S.S. Barcelona.* 1968 AMC 331).

> When a vessel sinks at a dock in clear weather, a presumption of unseaworthiness arises.
>
> —*(Charles Rosenburg v. Maritime Ins. Co. Ltd.* 1968 AMC 1609).

> Sinking in calm water raises a presumption that a vessel was unseaworthy and the burden is on the assured to prove her seaworthy, or that the cause of the sinking was within the Inchmaree clause.

—*(Capital Coastal Corp. et. Al. v. Hartford Fire Ins. Co.* 1974 AMC 2039)

While referencing the above it is also important to note that wear and tear is **not** covered under any marine insurance policy. There is another interesting aspect concerning the evaluation of claims and losses which is known as **Blind-Eye-Knowledge**. But first let's take a look at the basic criteria of Seaworthiness 101. Frequently yacht surveyors are asked to include in their report whether or not the vessel is seaworthy and in most cases they refuse. During trials in District Courts in San Juan, Miami, Baltimore and New York presiding judges have asked marine surveyors whether or not they had considered a vessel as seaworthy. One particular such incident happened in San Juan in the late 1990's when a Lloyd's Agent was testifying against certain underwriters at Lloyd's. As the Lloyd's Agent had personally inspected the vessel in question on a number of previous occasions the Magistrate broached the seaworthiness issue eliciting a negative response from the illustrious Lloyd's Agent who said that no one can or should ever state whether a vessel is seaworthy. It was a dumb answer that the judge immediately took note of. Let's step back and take a closer look at exactly how 'Seaworthiness' is defined.

According to the UK Marine Insurance Act, in a voyage policy there is an implied warranty that at the commencement of the voyage the ship shall be seaworthy for the purpose of the particular adventure insured (Sect.39) The law of the United States gives a wide berth to the implied warranty of seaworthiness. In the case of voyage policies which simply means the vessel is insured while it undertakes a voyage from say Miami to San Juan, it has been held that the assured is bound not only to have his vessel seaworthy at the commencement of the voyage but also to keep her seaworthy, so far as it depends on himself and his agents throughout the voyage. In Time policies, the assured's obligation is more limited. Although there is an implied warranty of seaworthiness at the time of attachment of the insurance the courts have said that there is not the usual warranty of seaworthiness but only the implied condition "that the vessel is in existence as such at the commencement of the risk, capable of navigation, and safe, whether at sea or in port at the commencement of the risk and seaworthy when she first sails, or, if at sea, had sailed seaworthy, and is safe." In England, with a time policy, there is no implied warranty that the ship shall be seaworthy at any stage of the adventure, but where, with the privity of the assured, the ship is sent to sea in an unseaworthy state, the insurer is not liable for any loss attributable to unseaworthiness (Sect. 39). A Time Policy is just that a policy that's issued for a specific time period, normally 12 months. A Voyage Policy covers a specific voyage. In simple terms under English law and practice if the owner had reason to believe that the vessel was unseaworthy and deliberately refrained from examination which would have turned the belief into knowledge, the insurer is not liable for any loss *attributable* to *unseaworthiness*. In the United States, a sort of negative, modified warranty was established in *Saskatchewan Government Insurance Office v. Spot Pak, Inc.* (1957 AMC 655) that, after attachment of the policy, the assured will not, from bad faith or neglect, knowingly permit the vessel to break ground in an unseaworthy condition. I'll address the issue of **blind-eye-knowledge** in the following pages.

Seaworthiness: *There is an implied warranty in every policy that the vessel is seaworthy at the commencement of the voyage or the attachment of the insurance. That is, the vessel must be reasonably fit in all respects, including the hull, equipment, stores, bunkers, crew and officers, to encounter the ordinary perils contemplated for the voyage and her intended use. If the vessel is in port she must be reasonably fit to encounter the perils of the port.*

In dealing with commercial vessels and this would include charter boats carrying passengers, the doctrine of seaworthiness incorporation into maritime law occurred in 1903 with the United States Supreme Court case concerning *The Osceloa*. The Supreme Court held that ship owners owe a duty to seamen to provide a seaworthy vessel. A vessel will be considered seaworthy only when all of its appurtenances and crew are reasonably fit for their intended purpose. The duty to provide a seaworthy vessel is absolute. The determination of seaworthiness is a straightforward, boiler-plate decision that any trained and competent marine surveyor should and must make. Underwriters and in some cases the courts require this information. In the above referenced San Juan case the magistrate ruled in favor of the underwriters at Lloyd's, but not before adding that the credibility of the Lloyd's Agent was effectively destroyed by his admission on cross examination that he failed to document his theory with photographs. As the Judge deemed the testimony of the Lloyd's Agent as somewhat less than truthful, maybe this was just a nice way of saying that he lied. For little more than personal enrichment the Lloyd's Agent had prostituted himself, testified falsely under oath and engaged in nefarious conduct against the genuine interests of the London insurance market. The underwriters told me that they intended to file a complaint with the Lloyd's Committee suggesting that it was contrary to the interests of the Market to have Lloyd's Agents testifying against Lloyd's underwriters especially in cases that touched on fraudulent behavior by the assureds. Whether they did this or not I can't say, but in any case the word spread quickly throughout the City that there was a problem in Puerto Rico and the assignments for the Lloyd's Agent appeared to decline. If the underwriters in fact did file the complaint nothing more was ever heard about it. No doubt in their normal fashion the Lloyd's Agency System quietly swept the matter under their tarnished carpet.

On the 18th of January 2001 the House of Lords rendered in, Opinions of the House of Lords of Appeal for Judgment in the Cause of: Manifest Shipping Company Limited (Respondents) v. Uni-Polaris Shipping Company Limited and Others (Appellants) [2001] UKHL 1.

The full text of the document by the Honorable Lordships is too long and may not be of interest to all the readers of this book, but can be downloaded from the Internet[1]. The legal issue of **blind-eye-knowledge** came up in a claim for damages where expert witnesses provided evidence to the Court that clearly established that the owners of a vessel had full knowledge of the unseaworthy condition of the vessel yet sent her to sea in an unseaworthy state. Due to the unseaworthy condition of the vessel damages were incurred that had the vessel been seaworthy would not have occurred. I believe the comments by Lord Scott of Foscote clearly

---

1.   www.parliment.the-stationery-office.co.uk Go to Judgments Session 2000-01

described blind-eye-knowledge in his summary leading to the dismissal of the Appeal. For this reason I have included excerpts from his presentation that address Section 39(5) of the Marine Insurance Act 1906 where, with the privity of the assured, the ship is sent to sea in an unseaworthy state.

> "A contract of marine insurance is a contract based upon the utmost good faith and, if the utmost good faith be not observed by either party, the contract may be avoided by the other party."

The original presiding judge in this case expressed his conclusion on the critical issue of privity:

> "I do find that there was blind eye knowledge on the part of the assured. The inadequate response to the earlier fires and the state of the *Star Sea* on 27 May [1990], demonstrate in my judgment that the assured did not want to know about her unseaworthiness in the relevant respects."

On 18 January 2001 Lord Steyn and Lord Hoffman dismissed the appeal.

Lime Street—In the Beginning

Nothing Succeeds Like Success......

It's not possible to speak of marine insurance without first drawing reference to the institution known simply as LLOYD'S or the MARKET. Following the Great Fire of London commercial centers began to develop further to the east principally around Tower Street and the area known as Eastcheap. Edward Lloyd opened his coffee house in the 1680's and most likely because of being near the Thames, it soon became a popular rendezvous of merchants involved with the insurance of ships and their cargoes. During the reign of Charles II in the 17th century, London coffee houses became a British tradition and each had a particular clientele. The medical profession preferred Child's where the bells from St. Paul's would frequently beheard, writers and poets were drawn to the Bedford in Covent Garden while City merchants gathered in the coffee houses sprinkled throughout the alleys around the Royal Exchange. Being an astute businessman Edward Lloyd encouraged the custom of the insurance trade as ship-owners knew that the Lloyd's coffee house would be the best place to find the underwriters. Evolving over the years the preeminence of Lloyd's existence still remains in the hands of syndicates, or groups of underwriters who provide insurance cover for a number of specialized risks including marine and aviation. Underwriters and in some cases their syndicates are highly motivated and competitive, they work effectively well together for the benefit of what is known as the Market. During the early period of Lloyd's there were no insurance companies as we know them today. Underwriters would personally guarantee commercial enterprises on an individual basis by signing their names underneath the policy wording. In signing below or underneath the policy wording, the description 'underwriter' has evolved for over 300 years. Over the years Lloyd's has gone through periods described as the best of times and equally the worst of times. The first crisis presented itself in 1769 when insurance was considered hardly more than gambling—a favorite pastime and 18th century obsession.

Lloyd's would have surely become extinct had not a group of creative underwriters convinced a waiter named Thomas Fielding to establish a coffee house in Popes Alley to compete with the domain created by Edward Lloyd. In the ensuing years space became a problem as the number of underwriters grew. To solve the problem a Committee was elected from 79 merchants, underwriters and brokers who each paid £100 into the Bank of England. The Committee would be tasked to find larger premises. Through the efforts of John Julius Angerstein who was never a member of the Committee; in 1774 Lloyd's moved to the Royal Exchange. In moving to the Royal Exchange the importance of the coffee houses diminished and was the primary factor in the creation of Lloyd's as we know it today. Much like the wood benches where the underwriters of years past sat to negotiate their risks and premiums, present day underwriters sit in 'boxes' where the brokers wait in line to present risks for binding and underwriters signatures. At Lloyd's the 'box' is the place of business where an underwriter who may in all probability be representing several hundred people, will have the authority for his syndicate to accept or decline each individual risk. The syndicate is made up of underwriting 'names' or members who provide, through their personal resources the financial capacity the underwriter needs to take on business. The broker presents the risk or request for cover which may be for an individual yacht or a fleet of charter vessels to a number of underwriters. By presenting the risk to a number of underwriters each will then have the opportunity to opt for a percentage of the risk or decline involvement. Their respective percentage entitles the underwriter to that percentage of the premium and the same percentage of any loss. The underwriter who has the largest percentage of the risk generally becomes the 'lead' and is entitled to make the decisions on behalf of the others (underwriters) on any subsequent claims against the policy. A simple yacht policy could have a dozen or more underwriters on the slip with as little as 5% of the risk. The slip is a simple form that identifies the risk, the conditions and the signatures of the various underwriters who have accepted the risk. The 'slip' was frequently viewed as no more than a memorandum of the insurance contract, binding in honor only and not legally enforceable until a valid policy was issued. Admiralty lawyers took a different view and proved their point through high awards from sympathetic judges and juries.

The Salvage Association (old)

May it rest in peace......

The late J. Paul Getty once said that to succeed in business one only needed to find a need and fill it. Such commentary is a bit simplistic, but then J. Paul Getty had a few million in the bank when he said it so he's entitled to say whatever pleased him. About a 147 years ago, give or take a decade, a group of underwriting members at Lloyd's and a gaggle of marine insurance companies that had emerged in London were having problems in dealing with hull and cargo claims in the event of a casualty that was further a field than Liverpool or Glasgow. Thus in 1856 "The Association for the Protection of Commercial Interests as respects [for] Wrecked and Damaged Property" was formed to deal with the brigands and villains who were receiving ill-gotten gains from questionable claims. No doubt the Sheriff of Nottingham was busy with the likes of Robin Hood and his merry men and the term insurance fraud or fourth degree felony obviously hadn't yet been created by the judiciary in England or the United States. In 1867 the 'Association' (you've got the full name already) was incorporated by Royal Charter thus becoming a legal entity with full corporate status—what ever that's supposed to mean. The Association muddled on until October 1971 when some jolly chap no doubt figured that writing out the full name was taking too much ink and in prematurely wearing out his quill pen so he opted for a change. In an effort to appease her noble subjects as well as those of the *Save the Quill Pen Movement*, Her Majesty Queen Elizabeth II granted the 'Association' a new royal charter under the name of "The Salvage Association". At this sitting I won't go into the assorted functions of the multiple layers of the various offices of chairman, deputy chairman, general managers, deputy and assistant general managers, chief surveyors, chief accountants and of course "The Committee". This dinosaur of organizational excess soon took up 'suitable' premises in London and ensconced itself in luxurious offices in New York and other 'appropriate' locations around the globe. Who paid for these excesses—you, me and anyone else that had a marine policy or bought anything that was to be transported by sea. First the underwriters would be obliged to pick up the tab, but then promptly added the costs to everyone's policy as a *cost of doing business.*

Now there were no doubt a handful of former workers who did their damnedest to do a good job at a reasonable cost, but they were simply outnumbered by those who didn't. I recall a particular incident that occurred some years ago in the Dominican Republic where the Salvage Association (SA) had been appointed to deal with a casualty involving a large European yacht insured in London for a million or two. The SA always liked the descriptive ring of a **casualty** over a mere claim probably because it sounded chic allowing for justification of greater fees and unchallenged expenses. I happened to be in the country dealing with another claim but found it odd that in view of the high value the SA surveyor wasn't closely monitoring the salvage effort. When I stopped by to see how things were progressing (for academic interest) I was told by the salvage crew who fortunately worked well without oversight, that if I wanted to speak with the SA surveyor he could normally be found at the pub in town during the afternoon. I didn't wish to speak with him but did find him in the Pub sampling the local cerveza. It's is quite possible that I didn't come into contact with the right people, but during my frequent visits to London I rarely heard the underwriters speak positively about the Salvage Association or heard the organization praised as being cost effective. Over the years as underwriters' costs and expenses spiraled upwards (especially the legal fees) many London insurers simply stopped using the Salvage Association which drove the final nail in their Royal corporate coffin. In traveling throughout the world on various claims on behalf of underwriters I was frequently in contact with a number of these jolly chaps from the SA (the Quill Pen Movement had no doubt asked The Salvage Association to cut the name down even more). While I have no problem with traveling in a first class seat, staying in a suite at a local five star hotel or consuming a broiled lobster with a fine Chardonnay it's just that I don't feel its right that the underwriters should have to pick up the tab. Before the collapse of the Salvage Association (old) this type of luxurious behavior was common practice for SA surveyors, at least where I have local knowledge in the Caribbean and Latin America. Due to its openly scandalous disregard of common business sense and ignominious behavior the Salvage Association (old) continued to dig its own grave until it was effectively *brain-dead* by late 2000. By early 2001 it had clearly died something that should have happened shortly after the Wright Brothers took off from Kitty Hawk; if this had been the case we all would have saved a lot of money.

In March 2001 the Salvage Association (old) much like a cat with nine lives or the Phoenix rising from the ashes, was itself salvaged and came back to life as the Salvage Association (new) and part of the British Maritime Technology (BMT) Group. Recognizing that the basic principle and objectives of a salvage association was sound, it was obvious that such an enterprise and undertaking simply needed 21st century management skills. It's still a bit premature to tell, but it's possible that under the direction of a responsible and profit motivated corporate entity such as the BMT a new and viable Salvage Association may emerge from the ashes and be able to shed the dubious 147 year history of its namesake. The Salvage Association (old) did prove one of the basic principles of Business 101 expounded by those institutions offering MBAs, being big and old doesn't guarantee survival. I wish BMT every success in their endeavors.

The Lloyd's Agency System

Image over Substance......

Lloyd's Agents have historically reported to their London elders the movement of ships throughout the world, weather conditions and other information deemed to be of importance to the Market, which was no doubt a noble task during the age of Nelson and Hornblower. Other than these transitory duties while ships laded with tea from India or silk from China made their perilous voyages to Liverpool or London, Lloyd's agents in the West Indies became an exclusive gentlemen's club that in some jurisdictions changed its membership like the sheets in an airport Holiday Inn. However, in today's world of shipping and high speed communications there really is little to be said about the Lloyd's Agency System other than it's old. I should however, add that it has been very profitable to a number of current and former Lloyd's Agents (at least in the Caribbean and Latin America) who have defrauded underwriters with amongst other cons, declaring yachts as total losses when they weren't, acting for assureds while they were acting for underwriters, and accepting gratuitous commissions from salvers and from assureds for favorably settling their claims contrary to insurers interests. One example of these excesses occurred following a recent hurricane when a local Lloyd's agent was said to have received so much money under-the-table he was able to purchase a US$250,000.00

home in the Dominican Republic—for cash. I first met this wannabe Lloyd's Agent after he had fled New York to take up residence on a neighboring Island during the same period that I was busy setting up an office in Philipsburg on the island of Sint Maarten; he was unemployed and looking for work. He eventually got an entry level job with a firm that represented insurers in London; a short time later his employer discovered he was pilfering the office files and selling confidential information to a ship owner who happened to be in litigation with the same London underwriters the firm represented. Deciding there was a thief in the office he was promptly fired. I met another of these depraved clowns whom I will call Joops, when he arrived in Sint Maarten, Netherlands Antilles looking for work after a less than illustrious sojourn with one of the Dutch cruise lines. Joops bounced from trying to make a living as a compass adjuster, then after a short stay at the Port Authority he anointed himself a marine surveyor.

No one really knows exactly why, but most likely in desperation to find someone, anyone to fill the void he was subsequently appointed the Lloyd's Agent in Sint Maarten. Joops hadn't received any training as a marine surveyor nor was he the most proficient while he tried to learn a bit about yachts or for that matter ships. Joops had no effect on my practice but was miffed because European and London underwriters would instruct me to carry out their work rather than use him, the local Lloyd's Agent. I was told that the underwriters were also a bit concerned that as a side-line Joops was acting as an insurance broker and selling marine insurance in addition to insisting that only he perform the condition and valuation surveys on the yachts he was selling insurance to. Joops no doubt believed his dual role was justified as on-the-job-training; however, being quite proper English gentlemen the underwriters in London didn't feel that the obvious conflict of interest demonstrated proper ethical conduct. I was told that the underwriters reported the unethical conduct to the Committee at Lloyd's, but the Committee did nothing. In February 1998 a Dutch passenger ship the SWAN VAN MAKKUM went aground at Sandy Island, Anguilla, British West Indies. The vessel's master Captain

Willem Sligting called for tug assistance to pull his lightly grounded ship free from the sandy beach. His call was answered by Captain Harry, owner of the tug St. John who believed he could free the Swan at a cost of $500.00 per hour. The two captains agreed the effort would take about 10 hours, which included the Tug's travel time to and from Sint Maarten. The $5,000.00 towage charge would be paid by Captain Sligting and reimbursed by his Dutch insurers, however, before the St. John could undertake the tow she developed engine problems and passed the tow to Captain John Miller, owner of the tug St. Ven. I have known John Miller for a number of years and found him to be an honest and responsible salver. Captain Miller pulled the Swan free, but then submitted a bill of $25,000.00 for the effort. When Captain Sligting objected to the outrageous charge he received a call from Joops the infamous Lloyd's Agent in Sint Maarten threatening to arrest the Swan if the $25,000.00 wasn't paid immediately. Captain Sligting couldn't get an answer from the Lloyd's Agent as to why he had involved himself when the matter didn't concern Joops or Lloyd's, he then contacted his insurance broker in Holland to report what appeared to be nothing more than a blatant attempt of extortion.

After receiving a menacing call from Joops the nefarious Lloyd's Agent, and Mr. Ronald Drupsteen of Kuiper Verzekeringen B.V. the Dutch brokers, Mr. Drupsteen contacted Esma Den Drijver Expertise BV who in turn instructed me to find out what was going on. Joop followed up his telephone call with a fax to the Dutch brokers advising that the salver (John Miller) wouldn't meet with me demanding that the Swan's insurers deal direct and only with him. Now you can ask an insurer to use your services, but making such a demand really isn't the best approach. To avoid having the Swan arrested while I attempted to find out what was going on I suggested that the vessel be moved from the jurisdiction of the Dutch side of Sint Maarten to the French side. Captain Sligting moved the ship the next day. What I subsequently learned was that Joops was to be paid a commission on the amount of salvage money he could extort from the Swan's insurers. Joops didn't want me to meet with the salver because if I was able to negotiate a reasonable salvage fee I would be taking a percentage of the proceeds out of Joops dirty pockets. After the Swan had been moved to the safety of Marigot on the French side of Saint Martin, the pressure Joops was exerting in threatening to have the vessel arrested no longer existed. While I knew John Miller, he had really been more of an acquaintance than a friend. The boating community in the Caribbean is a fairly tight group and while you may not know each of them intimately, you probably will know the person, his business or his boat. When I lived in St. Thomas I had a morning radio show on the local CBS affiliate station; *Shooting the Breeze* aired at 8:30 every morning and dealt with pertinent marine issues affecting the area. Because of my radio program many people may not have known me personally, but knew the name Ed Geary giving me the pleasure of meeting many of my listeners in my travels throughout the islands. When I called the salver to arrange a meeting to discuss the salvage of the SWAN VAN MAKKUM, John was a bit reserved saying that Joops told him he was waiting to hear back from underwriters and that he shouldn't meet with me. John confirmed that Joop had told him to demand a $25,000.00 payment as he would apply the pressure to get them to pay because he was "The Lloyd's Agent". John also confirmed that Joops was getting a cut from the salvage award and this was the reason he was keeping the pressure on for the full $25,000.00. I met with the salver on February 27th at a restaurant at Simpson Bay in St. Maarten. I explained that underwriters were quite willing to pay a reasonable settlement, but if this wasn't possible then they would invoke arbitration in London. I pointed out a number of issues that John should consider: the Swan van Makkum was no longer in Dutch territorial waters and therefore the vessel could not be arrested or detained. If any attempt was made to have the vessel arrested in French waters (which is far more difficult), with no passengers on board she could sail within 30 minutes to international waters. On the other hand if we couldn't reach an agreement then John's salvage company would be required to place funds in escrow and we'd all meet up for arbitration in London. It was obvious to both of us that Joops, the Lloyd's Agent in St. Maarten wasn't exactly honest. He'd shaken-down John for a piece of the salvage pie and was now trying to extort money from the Swan's underwriters. I was determined to stop Joops from completing his extortion plan. The salver acknowledged that he only wanted a fair compensation for his successful efforts and did not want to wait, possibly for years before the matter was arbitrated in London or get involved with monies held in bond along with the obvious legal fees he would incur. The Swan's underwriters in Holland had given me full authority to negotiate a settlement and close the matter so their assured could get back to the business of being a passenger ship without the fear of being arrested. The salver agreed to disassociate himself from Joops and eventually agreed to a full and final payment of $20,000.00. When considering the original $5,000.00 amount I had hoped for a lesser settlement, but accepted $20,000.00 on behalf of insurers. The Lloyd's Agent had totally compromised underwriter's interests and even though the $20,000.00 was still piracy, it provided closure. A short time after the Swan Van Makkum case was closed Erik den Drijver of Den Drijver Expertise of Amsterdam told me that he knew the name Joops from an earlier cargo fraud case that had occurred in Holland involving a yacht named the s/y White Heather. I knew the White Heather as I had been involved in the investigation into the vessel's dismasting in the British Virgin Islands a few years earlier. Sensing that something was wrong when the vessel arrived as damaged deck cargo with a falsified bill of lading at Rotterdam, Erik had notified the Dutch police who seized the White Heather and made a number of arrests. Erik den Drijver was certain that the Joop in St. Maarten was the same Joop in the fraud case of the White Heather in Holland; could it be that the Lloyd's Agent in Sint Maarten was a fugitive from justice? Interesting…Yet another Lloyd's agent in St. Thomas is reported to have disappeared with an estimated $200,000.00 of underwriter's money. Well that pretty much gives you an idea of an organization (at least their Caribbean clowns) whose credo is *Fidentia* and describes itself, "A unique Organisation Spanning the World". There is no question they were unique but only for the malfeasance and corruption that has permeated the Lloyd's Agency System like warm beer flowing through the cracks of a leaking keg. As I said previously, the Lloyd's Agency System is old and nothing more. An even more recent case of malfeasance and incompetence involved the Lloyd's Agents in Brazil and Paraguay when they reported that certain containers hadn't been opened and pilfered when in fact they had been opened and pilfered. When pressed, the explanation they gave was that they hadn't understood insurer's instructions. A suitable title for the legacy of Lloyd's Agents may be one of *Dumb & Dumber*. Anyone who has a boat, yacht, ship or insures cargo that is shipped on the ground, in the air or on the sea, unfortunately has paid dearly for the malfeasance of these sanctimonious buffoons. In dealing with claims over the last number of years I have found that under normal circumstance about half of the claims filed have been straightforward fortuitous losses except when losses are incurred as a result of a hurricane or other natural disaster. When a disaster strikes, fraudulent claims sometimes increase by 25% or more. Hurricanes, storms with subsequent losses bring out the best in people and unfortunately the worst. It also becomes feeding time for a number of unscrupulous Lloyd's Agents.

> Nothing in life is more exhilarating as to be shot at without result.
>
> —1888 Winston Spencer Churchill, The Malakand Field Force

Marine insurance policies provide cover for ignorance, inexperience, foolishness and sometimes just plain stupidity. As I have mentioned previously marine insurance policies do not cover wear and tear or the willful misconduct of the assured. Simply put, if you have a loss where the cause (*causa proxima*) is directly related to normal wear and tear of a particular part or component, like the mast falls down because of rusted wire or terminal fittings, it's excluded. Willful misconduct means that if you burn or sink your boat because you can't make your monthly alimony or other payments the loss won't be covered. If it can be proven that you did the dirty deed and committed fraud you may be fined or go to jail. In addition to hull and machinery (H&M) claims and Property and Indemnity (P&I) claims I have also been involved with a number of cargo claims. While the use of containers has helped reduce the theft of merchandise sealed inside, it has also created a new breed of thieves who in gaining access to steal the high value contents may also provide terrorists a perfect method to ship

C4 explosives, dirty bombs, poisonous chemicals and gases, etc., etc., etc. A recent case in Port of Spain, Trinidad found repeated thefts of high value liquor from containers that had their seals intact. I became involved when I was asked to inspect a 40' container that had been shipped from England to St. Thomas, U.S. Virgin Islands through Port of Spain, Trinidad. When it arrived at the consignee's warehouse in Charlotte Amalie in St. Thomas the door seal was intact and had not been broken, yet 488 cases of liquor had been removed. My investigation found that the left door had been opened by simply bending a small retainer plate on the right door; the left door could then be opened without challenging the seal on the right door. In removing the whisky which had been secured in the forward part of the container, the thieves simply walked over the low priced gin secured near the rear doors. Normally when thieves penetrate containers they sometimes remove and reweld the doors hinges, drill out the bolts holding the retaining pins, all of which can be easily seen. This group in Trinidad obviously found that 5 minutes to bend a small plate was quicker and far more efficient than the normal methods of entry to a sealed container. The case is now in the hands of Homeland Security (US Customs) and hopefully won't make the evening news as a result of a dirty bomb wiping out half of Miami. When containers are now shipped from Europe the problem has been resolved, at least for the present time as shippers now require that seals be secured on both the right and left container doors.

Over the years I have had a number of interesting cases involving salvers negligence, repairers who inflate repair costs to include the assureds deductible, repair or replacement costs for parts that weren't damaged, costs for expensive electronic equipment that had been taken off the vessel before the loss, or was never there in the first place and claims submitted by persons who didn't own the insured vessel. Once the fraud has been exposed most of the claims have been resolved with the claims being withdrawn. Others have resulted in the perpetrators being quietly brought to justice saving a number of underwriters a few Dollars, Pounds and Euros in the process. A case that took place in the southern Caribbean involved a

$200,000.00 yacht that had been stolen in Sint Maarten. A short time after the yacht disappeared she was sighted on the Dutch island of Curacao then later turned up in Venezuela. In monitoring the vessel's movements after the theft I subsequently learned that I was not the only person keeping an eye on the yacht, it was also under surveillance of other law enforcement agencies in Venezuela. After receiving a call from the French police I learned that the European occupants of the vessel were using the yacht as a control point in a conspiracy to purchase Colombian cocaine for delivery by ship to Europe through West Africa. The participants included a number of Europeans and members of a Russian crime group. This became known as the case of The French Connection II. It was an interesting case that involved a lot of legwork, investigative research and a bit of luck. I've always been somewhat careful about the luck factor as I firmly believe that in most cases a good investigator creates his own good luck. The experienced investigator knows that to be successful you have to doggedly follow your hunches, carefully categorize all your information, establish motive and opportunity and then profile your targets. By doing so the successful investigator creates what others will later describe as good luck. The case of the French Connection II had all the ingredients of a good mystery novel. After finding the stolen yacht in Venezuela I placed her under surveillance with the assistance of my fellow officers in the Venezuelan Coastguard. What I wasn't aware of at the time was that my Coastguard surveillance team had also been placed under surveillance by French narcotics agents operating out of the French embassy in Caracas. I only learned of this a short time later when I received a call from police commissioner Jacque Mafre head of the French narcotics task force. Jacque told me that the French authorities knew I was watching the yacht, waiting for the right opportunity to swoop and recover her for insurers; he asked if I could meet with him at the French embassy in Caracas the following week. Jacque told me that the stolen yacht was being used by French, German and Russian drug dealers as a refuge where they were developing a plan to orchestrate the movement of a ship load of cocaine from Cartagena, Columbia that would rendezvous with a Russian cargo ship that was presently in Pampatar on the Venezuelan island of Margarita. The Russian, German and Italians nationals on board the yacht were wanted by INTERPOL for drug trafficking and the French had warrants outstanding in France for not only for trafficking, but also murder. While I wanted to assist the French authorities I told Jacque I wouldn't be willing to risk losing the yacht, which I didn't feel would appeal to the insurers. I agreed to pull back my surveillance team if this could be taken over by the French. It was agreed that the French Narcs as part or their surveillance would covertly place a satellite tracking device on the hull which would be monitored every 6 hours. If the vessel moved from the Macuto Sheraton Marina, Jacque would immediately call me to advise of the vessel's movements, especially if she sailed eastward to the Atlantic. Everything went as planned until a week later when the yacht left the Macuto Sheraton and sailed east on a course towards Isla Margarita. The next day I was on a plane to Venezuela. Overlooking the harbor in Pampatar the French had set up a command post with listening devices so sophisticated that we could hear every conversation inside the yacht down to the flushing of the toilet in the aft cabin. When the occupants sat in the cockpit they were repeatedly photographed through telephoto lenses with such definition that they could detail the tattoos on the arm of one of the Russians. So typical of the French police they had agents that in addition to French were fluent in Russian, Italian, and German. The next day when the drug traffickers had completed their arrangements for the ships to transfer the cocaine it was time to close in. Watching from the penthouse the Venezuelan Coastguard patrol boats encircled the yacht and arrested all those on board. Simultaneously heavily armed patrol craft of the Venezuelan Navy boarded the Russian and Colombian ships before the first kilo was transferred. The entire operation took less than an hour without a shot being fired. We celebrated that night like only the French know how. I received a letter of commendation from the French government for our joint cooperative efforts that lead to the seizure of a shipload of narcotics and the arrest of the traffickers. As a result of the successful outcome of the case in 1996 the IAMI named me the Investigator of the Year.

The Andersen Conspiracy
Arthur Andersen et al

You can fool some of the people some of the time,
but not all the people all of the time…

In the fall of 1999 Mr. Doran McClellan of Arthur Andersen's San Francisco office was interviewed by Ms. Allison Smith for an article that appeared in the Lloyd's List in London on December 22nd 1999. The newspaper article, captioned ARTHUR ANDERSEN SHIP VALUATION LAUNCH touted the expertise and experience of this global accountancy firm in the valuation of commercial ships. In the article Mr. McClellan stated, "So far we have valued 16 ships, most notably cable laying vessels, container and chemical carriers…… Banks can request an 'abridged' valuation of a ship by asking for some of the stages to be overlooked. This can cut down on how much the deal is worth. In contrast to the unregulated sale and purchase broking business the Arthur Andersen team are certified by the American Society of Appraisers. A rigorous set of examinations must be sat for qualification." The only thing that McClellan was right about was the rigorous set of examinations. I and the other eleven accredited senior appraisers of ships went through the examination process, McClellan and the Arthur Andersen team didn't. McClellan or his 'team' didn't have any qualifications or hold the certifications for the valuation of a row boat much less a ship. The United Kingdom and espe-cially London is the respected and unquestionable leader of all things mar-itime. As a daily newspaper the *Lloyd's List* has attained a reputation for accuracy and reliability almost to the level of the Bible when it comes to marine insurance, shipping and banking. When I first became aware of McClellan's promotion of himself and Arthur Andersen's ship valuation team I quietly researched the qualifications of McClellan with the Ameri-can Society of Appraisers (ASA) in Washington. The ASA confirmed that McClellan, Arthur Andersen or his team did not possess appraisal qualifi-cations for yachts, ships or for that matter anything that floats. The *Lloyd's List* and their reporter Ms. Allison Smith had been conned by McClellan and the now defunct Arthur Andersen LLP. Bear in mind this scenario was exposed shortly before Andersen's indictment for the firm's criminal activ-ities in the ENRON debacle.

Being a subscriber and reader of the Lloyd's List and believing they would like to know that they had published false/fraudulent information I contacted Tony Gray, a financial journalist and Julian Bray, the editor of this Bible of shipping. I suggested that to maintain the integrity of the Lloyd's List a retraction and correction of Arthur Andersen's fraudulent misrepresentations was worthy of consideration. I was first told by Tony Gray, the financial reporter that a correction and retraction would be pub-lished as requested by Mr. Edwin Baker the executive Director of the ASA in Washington. I was later surprised to find that Julian Bray the editor of the *Lloyd's List* had no interest in exposing the Arthur Andersen Conspir-acy even if it were to be buried at the bottom of the last page. They had published an article that was false and fraudulent yet had no interest in admitting their own error. They were however, interested in quickly cover-ing their royal posteriors and sweeping it as far under the carpet as possi-ble. As part of Julian Brays' royal sweep, Allison Smith, the reporter who had written the Arthur Andersen story quickly disappeared from the pay-roll of the *Lloyd's List*. I had first reported the breach of unethical conduct, misrepresentation and fraud committed by McClellan and Arthur Ander-sen LLP to Ed Baker, the executive director of the American Society of

Appraisers on February 8, 2000 who wrote a letter of admonishment to McClellan. In Baker's letter he demanded that McClellan have a correction printed in the next or subsequent issue of the *Lloyd's List* that he, McClellan was not certified in marine survey and that the ASA does not certify 'teams'. Mr. Baker further noted, "You may also include in the correction that Arthur Andersen LLP is an affiliate firm of the American Society of Appraisers, provided that no implication of accreditation, designation, or appraisal qualification is made." It was obvious that McClellan and the Arthur Anderson *gang* sorry, team, had been caught in a conspiracy to defraud ship owners and was told to set the record straight. What happened after this was quite amazing. In exposing the fraud I publicized the fraudulent acts with fellow members of the Society and filed a formal ethics complaint with the ASA in Washington. Both McClellan and Arthur Andersen's corporate headquarters ignored Baker's letter of admonishment and the ASA's demand of retraction. The following week I received an e-mail and two anonymous phone calls late at night where the callers said I might not be able to publicly expose the Andersen Conspiracy if I were dead. Undeterred I continued my efforts to expose these fraudsters throughout the year 2000.

On January 5, 2001 I received New Year's greetings from John M. Touhy, Esq. from the law offices of Mayer, Brown & Platt in Chicago, and mouthpieces for the Andersen fraudsters. Touhy demanded that I immediately cease and desist from making defamatory statements concerning the Andersen Conspiracy or they would sue me. McClellan and the firm of Arthur Andersen were nothing more than artful crooks, fraudsters and racketeers engaged in a criminal conspiracy to defraud, and their own documents proved it. If Mr. Touhy wanted to sue me—I told him to go ahead. The callers didn't kill me and Touhy didn't sue me. However, I vigorously continued my campaign to expose the fraudsters in the interest of bringing these crooks to justice. It was clear that the corruption at Arthur Andersen LLP wasn't limited to the dung at McClellan's level, but went all the way to the top. I know this because I individually emailed and telephoned the various managing directors, senior partners and the chairman of Arthur Andersen personally. As in the case of ENRON, when the criminal indictments were handed down, Arthur Andersen's senior management denied any knowledge of the fraud and scattered like rats leaving a sinking ship. Arthur Andersen LLP dissolved like sugar in hot tea while Andersen Consulting changed its name to Accenture moved offshore. I pursued the ethics complaint that I had filed with the ASA, but kept getting stonewalled. I contacted John Bakken who was chairman of the ASA's ethics committee who I believed was a friend (he wasn't) to find out what was going on. Nothing. Why? The ethics committee of the American Society of Appraisers was stuffed with Arthur Andersen cronies. McClellan and Arthur Andersen had engaged in a criminal conspiracy to defraud which had been documented by the Lloyd's List article and later confirmed in Ed Baker's letter of February 8, 2000. Any member of a professional organization that has an ethics code and a method of dealing with ethics complaints should feel confident that ethics violations will be dealt with fairly, expediently and without prejudice. This would have been the case had the ethics committee been chaired by a forthright and honorable individual and not compromised and prejudiced by committee members who were self serving employees of Arthur Andersen. Clearly if the officers of the ASA acted properly they would compromise their *cash-cow* of membership's fees and dues received from hundreds of Arthur Andersen's employees. It wasn't a great surprise that my ethics complaint against the fraudsters was summarily dismissed. But keep reading there's still more to come. The Arthur Andersen fraudsters hadn't stopped me with their death threats, a lawsuit to silence me or in dismissing my ethics complaint with the ASA so they took another course.

One of McClellan's cronies in Andersen's San Francisco office, a John R. Gasiorowski, filed an ethics complaint against me for 'Unprofessional Conduct toward another Appraiser.' I don't know Gasiorowski and have never met him. In accordance with the Constitution and by-laws of the American Society of Appraisers I had exposed a member of the organization who the ASA itself acknowledged was a fraudster, but because of Arthur Andersen's corrupting influence, the ASA refused to take any action. McClellan's buddy Gasiorowski crawled from under his rock and became the latest pawn in Arthur Andersen's effort to silence me. The Andersen/ASA conspiracy then deepens; if they couldn't silence me the conspirators would have me thrown out of the ASA; by expelling me from the membership I wouldn't be able to pursue my complaints against the Andersen Gang. Not to be outmaneuvered I then filed an ethics complaint against each individual member of the ASA ethics committee, the ASA's president Richard Amoling and all the members of the board of directors of the American Society of Appraisers. The complaint cited the ASA and its officers and directors for failure to adhere to the protocols referenced in the Society's Constitution and By-laws. In my complaint against the officers I noted that the American Society of Appraisers has a legal and moral responsibility to protect the public, users of professional appraisal services and the membership against unethical and unprofessional conduct. In willfully engaging in the cover-up of the offenses, public opinion and ultimately the judiciary would determine based on the hard evidence, that the ASA and its officers and directors had knowingly become a party with Arthur Andersen in a conspiracy to defraud the public. Nothing further was ever heard from the fraudster's mouthpieces in Chicago. No doubt after choking on my authenticated charges of the breach of fiduciary duty and malfeasance demonstrated by the officers and directors of the ASA, Their attorney in Washington called my lawyer in an effort to quietly resolve our 'differences'. I had become a member and qualified as an Accredited Senior Appraiser of the American Society of Appraisers on April 8th 1983. I had faithfully served the organization including a number of terms as president of the Puerto Rico and Virgin Islands chapters in addition to being named the regional director for the Caribbean. The ASA dropped the ethics complaint against me for exposing the fraud, swept the matter under the carpet and closed the file. I didn't close my file.

Not to be dissuaded in the exposure of the fraud committed by the Andersen gang on June 15, 2000 I filed an ethics complaint (BHS 00-026) against Arthur Andersen LLP with the American Institute of Certified Public Accountants (AICPA). In spite of the undeniable evidence of fraudulent misconduct I received a letter dated November 9, 2000 stating, "Based on a review of the complaint conducted in accordance with established Joint Enforcement Procedures, it has been determined that the allegation(s) in your complaint would not constitute a violation of the Code of Professional Conduct. Therefore the AICPA's Professional Ethics Division will not initiate an investigation of the complaint at this time and accordingly has made no determination and obtained no information with respect to the matter other than supplied by you." The letter was signed by Vincent A. DiBlanda, Technical Manager of the Professional Ethics Division. What a nice touch. Arthur Andersen engages in a conspiracy to defraud its clients by misrepresenting its professional qualifications and the AICPA, without an investigation, obtains no information, but determinations that fraudulent misrepresentation of professional qualifications doesn't violate the AICPA's Code of Conduct. The position and lack of action taken by the AICPA were clearly flawed and prejudicial to public interest. In the passing of the Sarbanes-Oxley Act, Washington put a stop to their malfeasance. Justice was however served when soon thereafter Arthur Andersen was indicted in the ENRON criminal conspiracy. Their employees quickly scurried in hopes of finding new employers who would hopefully be willing to overlook where they came from. McClellan and Arthur Andersen's San Francisco office soon disappeared. I'm still a senior member of the Society and hold accredited senior status until 2010. The ASA has quietly sealed the file. I'm not bitter just disappointed in how an important and once respected professional organization like the ASA can demonstrate such a flagrant lack of responsible leadership and become totally corrupted by a nefarious gang such as those at Arthur Andersen LLP. It wasn't necessary for me to pursue the fraudsters further because only a few weeks later the US Attorneys Office issued the indictments and criminal charges that ultimately removed forever, the blight and corruption perpetrated by the Arthur Andersen gang.

"…The main reason that the Sarbanes-Oxley Act was passed was to respond to the concerns of the American Public and Congress about major fraud in companies like Enron and WorldCom."

Even before ENRON, the Andersen fraudsters were developing new methods of deception.

Sale & Purchase   LLOYD'S LIST

Arthur Andersen ship valuation launch

Alison Smith

GLOBAL accountancy firm, Arthur Andersen, has launched an independent ship valuation business to rival the traditional ship-broker service and offer objectivity and accountability to the banking community.

"We feel that there is a great deal of business in offering investors and other financial institutions an approach that is more meaningful. What we can bring to the ship valuation table is our independence and expertise," Doran McClellan, head of the San Francisco based ship valuation team said.

"We do not buy and sell ships and the valuation is not provided to guarantee future business with a client. Consequently our objectivity is not jeopardised in any way.

In stark contrast to the sale and purchase broker's highly qualified 'estimate' Arthur Andersen provides a weighty report documenting how the value

was derived along with the risk factors.

While the team has typically found business at the high capital end of the spectrum Mr McClellan said that the market was opening up to business historically the broker's premise, "So far we have valued 16 ships, most notably cable laying vessels, containers and chemical carriers," he reported.

"Originally the service was mainly for tax-based structures such as leasing deals and so on but we are now seeing tanker and bulk carrier valuations filtering through to us."

Rather than a sole focus on the resale value based on a 'last done' deal on the sale and purchase markets, the Arthur Andersen methodology includes 'cost' and 'income' approaches. The 'cost' approach refers to how much a newbuilding replacement would cost minus physical deterioration and func-

tional deductions, while the 'income' method relates to how much an investor would pay.

"All three are used when we attach a value," Mr McClellan commented.

"As there would be contradictions when reconciling the results to a single number the relative importance of each method is weighted dependent on the type of ship and whether it has a charter attached."

"For example there is no real secondary market for cable ships so in the absence of comparable transactions the value would be derived on a combination of income and cost approaches" he explained, "however, for a bulk carrier we would look use a market approach, newbuilding ceilings and future earnings streams to provide a 'reality check' on the market value."

Mr McClellan admitted that in terms of fees the Arthur Ander-

sen service was considerably more costly than the brokers he said that the pricing structure was flexible enough not to deter customers.

"Banks can request an 'abridged' valuation of a ship by asking for some of the stages to be over-looked.

"This can cut down the cost depending on how much the deal is worth" he said.

In contrast to the unregulated sale and purchase broking business the Arthur Andersen team are certified by American Society of Appraisers. A rigorous set of examinations must be sat for qualification.

The venture represents one of the first attempts to apply corporate finance appraisal techniques to the shipping industry. Ship valuation is generally considered to be an 'art' rather than having any grounding in science in light of the volatility in value and concentration on asset play

22 Dec 1999

The above article appeared in the
Lloyd's List, London, England on December 22, 1999
In fraudulently misrepresenting their professional qualifications and illicit accreditation in the appraisal and valuation of ships, which they did not possess, Doran McClellan and Arthur Andersen engaged in a fraud that not only violated professional ethics but the public trust.

AMERICAN SOCIETY OF APPRAISERS

INTERNATIONAL HEADQUARTERS • P.O. Box 17285, Washington, DC 20041-0265 • (703) 478-2228 • Fax (703) 742-8471 • http://www.appraisers.org

Edwin W. Baker
Executive Director
Baker@appraisers.org

February 8, 2000

Mr. Doran V. McClellan, ASA
Arthur Andersen LLP
Spear Street Tower
1 Market Plaza
San Francisco, CA   94105

Dear Mr. McClellan:

The enclosed article by Alison Smith published in *Lloyd's List* has been brought to my attention by a member of the American Society of Appraisers (ASA). As a former member of ASA's Public Relations Committee, you are aware that the Society does not certify "teams." Also no mention was made in the article that you received your ASA designation in MTS/Machinery and Equipment.

Please have a correction to this article printed in the next or subsequent issue of *Lloyd's List* stating that ASA does not certify "teams" and that ASA does designate appraisers in MTS/Marine Survey but that your designation was received in MTS/Machinery and Equipment.

You also may include in the correction that Arthur Andersen LLP is an affiliate firm of the American Society of Appraisers, provided that no implication of accreditation, designation, or appraisal qualification is made.

After the correction is printed, please provide me with a copy. Thank you.

Sincerely yours,

Edwin W. Baker

Enclosure

cc:
Gerald L. Huether, ASA

**AMERICAN
SOCIETY OF
APPRAISERS**

A S A

INTERNATIONAL HEADQUARTERS • P.O. Box 17265, Washington, DC 20041-0265 • (703) 478-2228 • Fax (703) 742-8471 • http://www.appraisers.org

INTERNATIONAL ETHICS COMMITTEE

Chair:

John E. Bakken, ASA
Business Appraisal Associates, Inc.
P.O. Box 581
Granby, CO 80446-0581
Tel (970) 887-9563
Fax (970) 887-9569
E-mail jbakken@juno.com

Members:

Vern A. Blair, ASA
Blair Crosson Voyer
1650 Commerce Place
400 Burrard Street
Vancouver, BC 6VC 3A6
Canada
Tel (604) 684-6592
Fax (604) 684-9632
E-mail blair@taxsolve.com

Claire H. Donias, FASA
Arthur Andersen LLP
633 West Fifth Street
Los Angeles, CA 90071-2008
Tel (213) 614-6524
Fax (213) 614-6438
E-mail claire.h.donias@us.
   arthurandersen.com

Richard A. Hause, ASA
Marshall & Stevens, Inc.
1700 Market Street #1510
Philadelphia, PA 19103
Tel (215) 561-5600
Fax (215) 557-7280
E-mail ptshause@aol.com

Robert J. West, ASA
2681 Latham Drive
Sacramento, CA 95864
Tel (916) 973-1936
Fax (916) 973-0118
E-mail Robert.JWes@aol.com

June 23, 2000

Capt. E.S. Geary
Geary Associates
P.O. Drawer 1246
Fajardo, PR 00738-1246

Dear Capt. Geary:

At the last meeting of the Ethics Committee, the members of the committee voted to close the ethics complaint filed against Doran McClellan. We wish to thank-you for bringing this matter to the attention of the Committee.

The Committee, however, in its review of the case, was troubled by certain statements attributed to you that border on a violation of ethics code 5.1 Protection of Professional Reputation of Other Appraisers.

Please be more careful in the future.

Sincerely yours,

John E. Bakken, ASA

Chair, Ethics Committee

November 9, 2000

PERSONAL AND CONFIDENTIAL

Capt. E.S. Geary
Geary Associates
PO Drawer 1246
Fajardo, P.R. 00738

Re: BHS 00-026, Arthur Andersen, LLP

Dear Mr. Geary:

The AICPA's Professional Ethics Division has acknowledged your complaint against Arthur Andersen, LLP on June 15, 2000.

Based upon a review of the complaint conducted in accordance with established Joint Ethics Enforcement Procedures, it has been determined that the allegation(s) in your complaint would not constitute a violation of the Code of Professional Conduct.

Therefore the AICPA's Professional Ethics Division will not initiate an investigation of the complaint at this time and accordingly has made no determination and obtained no information with respect to the matter other than that supplied by you.

Sincerely,

Vincent A. DiBlanda
Technical Manager
Professional Ethics Division

American Institute of Certified Public Accountants
Harborside Financial Center, 201 Plaza Three, Jersey City, NJ 07311–3881 • (201) 938–3000 • (212) 318–0500 • fax (201) 938–3329 • www.aicpa.org
ISO 9001 Certified

The CPA. Never Underestimate The Value.®

Some Interesting Case Files

When you have eliminated the impossible,
whatever remains however improbable,
must be the truth.

—Sherlock Holmes
Sir Arthur Conan Doyle

The French Connection
Location of the Investigation: Dutch West Indies, Florida, Cayman Islands, Cuba

Following the theft of a high value yacht that was stolen from a charter fleet in Sint Maarten the operators of the vessel conducted a massive air search to the West, East and South of Philipsburg but were unsuccessful in locating the boat because they learned later the professional thieves were believed to have taken the unlikely course to the north towards the Atlantic Ocean. I received a full description of the vessel along with a request for assistance. Inquiries through the IAMI NETWORK of Law Enforcement and Special Investigators in the region produced negative results. Two months after the disappearance I received information about a Frenchman who said that he had knowledge of the theft and had, through a third party, been told where the vessel was located. In contacting the Frenchman, who we shall call Didier, he told me that he could lead me to the stolen yacht in return for a reward of 10% of the yacht's insured value which he said he knew was $500,000.00. After numerous discussions by phone it was agreed we would meet to discuss the recovery. During our first meeting in Florida Didier said that underwriters must first pay him the 10% reward before he would say where the vessel was to be found. I countered that any reward would only be based on the value of the vessel after its recovery and even though it may have been insured for a certain value it may not have retained that value. Didier said that "his friend" had seen the vessel and that it was in the same condition as it was when it had been stolen. I was interested and asked how Didier and his *friend* had known what the condition was when it was stolen? If he knew the prior condition this was obviously the *first connection* with Didier to the theft.

I suggested that we might place the reward funds in escrow with a bank or attorney and then we could together travel to the yacht; confirm its present condition and value, organize its return after which the "reward" would be released to Didier. Didier demanded that he be paid before he would lead me to the yacht. I declined the offer telling him I needed verifiable confirmation that this was the vessel I was seeking before any money changed hands. Didier became angry and said categorically that this was definitely the stolen Sint Maarten boat. As his information was supposedly coming from his friend, how could Didier definitely know this was the vessel? Had he seen the yacht? Didier's story then changed. Didier said his friend had first told him about the vessel and had actually gone to see and take a number of photos while it was at anchor; a possible *second connection.* Presenting the photograph Didier proudly said," you can see there is no denying that this is the yacht that was stolen from in front of Bobby's Marina in Sint Maarten on September 13th." The exact date of the theft or its location had never been published; the *third connection.* In closely examining the photos I observed that the hatches were open but did not immediately point this out to Didier. I agreed that yes it did appear to be the same make and type as the missing yacht but there are dozens of yachts of this type in the Caribbean so it may or may not be the one I had an interest in. I then pointed out the open hatches asking if someone was on the yacht now. "No", Didier said his friend had secured the vessel so it was safe, but had not gone onboard. Pressing the point that the hatches were open in the photograph, Didier became unnerved and then admitted that he had been on board; the *fourth connection*. The photograph of the vessel was important, but what was more important was what was around the yacht, the topography, sea state, trees, and the buildings that provided a picture of the area. Changing tactics I said that even though I would still need to make a positive ID to be certain that this was the vessel, I would agree to make arrangements for the payment of the reward to Didier. Upon hearing this, the Frenchman became relaxed and exhibited a broad smile. After it had been taken from Sint Maarten I had extended the search for the stolen vessel to Central and South America and throughout the Caribbean basin north to the Turks and Caicos Islands, but because of political problems had not included Cuba.

The photograph showed a West Indian type building situated near water that was a light blue and therefore shallow, the low coastline displayed scrub and small pines protruding from a sandy, coral ringed beach. The photo of the stolen vessel was either taken in the lower Bahamas, maybe an island in the Turks and Caicos that had been overlooked or on the South Coast of Cuba. Grand Turk and Provodenciales had been thoroughly searched in the last month so this area was deleted as a possible location. The boat was either somewhere in the Bahamas Out Islands or in Cuba. The only area in Cuba that matched the Photo was Cayo Largo on the southern coast. After the extensive interrogation of the target I felt confident that Didier had stolen the vessel and by limiting its present location to only two areas I continued to press Didier to reveal the exact location of the stolen yacht. I then decided to offer the target an opportunity to steal a bit more. Asking Didier questions about the yacht I found that he knew exactly how much fuel was on board, earlier problems with the port engine and other particulars that could only be known to the thief. The possible location was narrowed question by question about fuel, water and provisioning availability. I then flattered Didier by saying that he was obviously a very knowledgeable sailor asking if he would be willing for a generous fee, to return the yacht to its rightful owners in Sint Maarten.

Didier readily agreed asking how much? Well how many days will it take you to sail from where ever the vessel is now back to Sint Maarten? He responded with, "Eight days at the most because it's downwind from Philipsburg." Unwittingly Didier carelessly added that, "actually, the last time I did the trip we were coming from Sint Maarten it took six days". He jumped at the chance when I offered him $200.00 per day for the delivery. Two telephone calls to contacts in Havana confirmed the vessel was at Cayo Largo, Cuba. I ended the meeting with Didier saying that I would make arrangements for the payment of the money to his attorney in Fort Lauderdale agreeing to contact him in a few days to arrange for the delivery. Driving Didier and his female accomplice back to their seedy motel in Fort Lauderdale I took a number of photos of the pair (a pen recorder and shirt pocket camera is always standard equipment during the course of such an investigation). The photos would later be sent to INTERPOL. A British delivery crew was organized from Tortola and briefed on the mission to recover the yacht. Through Santo Domingo the delivery crew flew to Havana took the air shuttle to Cayo largo where they met with the Cuban Coastguard officer engaged by my contacts in Havana who paid him $3,000.00 U.S. Dollars to fuel and provision the yacht for the 143 nautical mile voyage south to the Cayman Islands.

The $3,000.00 paid unofficially to the Cuban Coastie represented his salary for a number of years, but was a bargain considering the $50,000.00 that Didier was attempting to extort for the return of the yacht. At the pre-arranged time the British crew were taken to the yacht and immediately set sail for George Town in the Cayman Islands. As the Cuban Coastguard official waved them off he raised his hands giving the crew a two thumbs-up. The stolen yacht was recovered undamaged. Before leaving, the British skipper using my photographs of the pair was able to confirm with the Port Captain's office that the Frenchman Didier and his female companion had brought the yacht to Cayo Largo six days after it had been stolen from Sint Maarten. The British delivery crew also obtained photocopies of their Passport photo pages which Didier had provided to the port Captain when they entered the Cuban port of Cayo Largo, the photocopies included their dates and place of Birth. The details were subsequently turned over to INTERPOL and the French Authorities. Didier and his companion were later apprehended on the island of Martinique in the French West Indies; after delivery arrangements were made the yacht was recovered and returned undamaged to its owners in Sint Maarten. Monsieur Didier made no further claims for a reward.

◆   ◆   ◆

There are times when the investigator has little to go on in the form of hard evidence and therefore must rely solely on instincts and hunches in pursuit of the truth. The target in this case knew too much about the stolen vessel and its condition, even down to what fuel was on board. With a sound local knowledge of the Caribbean Basin, reliable informants and in applying principles of psychology in pointed interrogation of the suspect, question by question the target drew a line that pin-pointed the exact location of the stolen yacht leading to its successful recovery.

Here Today/Gone Tomorrow or the Snatch & Grab Caper
Location of the Investigation: Cancun, Mexico and Miami, Florida

Once upon a time there was a marine finance group known as Horizon Credit. Under the regal guidance and noble leadership of the indisputable king of creative marine finance, John (Jack) Doyle, the company flourished, ultimately becoming an industry leader. Horizon, based in New Jersey, provided creative financing to major yacht dealerships, yacht brokers, yacht owning corporations and other affluent individuals. I had the pleasure to become involved with Jack Doyle when they expanded and began providing finance packages to customers in Puerto Rico and the U.S. Virgin Islands. Eduardo (Tati) Ferrer owner of the Villa Marina Yacht Harbour was one of Horizon's first big accounts in Puerto Rico. Along with the business from Villa Marina Yacht Sales and a Ms. Gonzalez, a San Juan yacht broker, who Jack said made most her sales while entertaining her clients in the forward cabin, Horizon grew from strength to strength. My professional and personal relationship with the management of the company grew as Horizon's influence quickly expanded throughout the United States. I was frequently called upon to testify as an expert in yacht valuation cases in bankruptcy courts in Texas, California and Florida. During one of my visits to Horizon's New Jersey offices I was told about a problem involving a 65' Hatteras sport fisherman. Horizon had a distant relationship with another financial group that carried the paper on the Hatteras and wasn't sure how to deal with the problem so they called Jack who suggested they ask me to look at the case. The vessel had mysteriously disappeared from her berth at a marina in Ft. Lauderdale two days after the owner of the boat had died. The widow had promptly reported the theft to the police and the loss to the insurers, which was the problem. The insurance policy had expired three months earlier and the now deceased owner hadn't submitted the renewal forms or paid the renewal premium. The insurance had been canceled, but the Bank hadn't been notified until after the vessel disappeared. The Bank had a serious problem and without insurance wanted their asset back. I accepted the case (or maybe the challenge would be a better choice of words) of locating and hopefully, recovering the stolen vessel.

The case was indeed daunting because those involved weren't exactly of the Mr. Nice Guy type. I soon learned that one of the players and the partner of the late Mr. Vasquez was *el jefe* of the Guadalajara Drug Cartel. No one ever had a problem with Don Francisco Marquez because he'd simply have his problems killed. Marquez clearly wasn't from Mr. Roger's neighborhood and was obviously a dangerous character. Don Francisco did have one nice side, he liked boats. He particularly liked his late partner's boat the *Costa Brava* and after deciding that as Pedro was no longer with us he wouldn't need his boat. If successful, the Bank would hopefully become a good client as was Horizon. Later, on at least three different occasions I seriously questioned the wisdom getting involved with the recovery of the Hatteras. After a case is closed and the dust settles I feel it's very important to look back and critique yourself at what could have been done better or maybe more effectively and which may be applied in future assignments. I've had the fun to work on a number of challenging and interesting cases that put your knowledge and skills to the test, but generally the cases haven't involved opponents that would have no hesitation in killing you. 'Here Today—Gone Tomorrow' was clearly one of my most fascinating cases. While some of the ground work took place in Miami most of the action was focused in Cancun, Mexico. Cancun is a relatively new tourist development located on Mexico's Caribbean coast and consists of a cluster of international luxury hotels, white sand beaches, charter boats, great restaurants and even better cantinas. The investigation was intensive but at the same time I also had a lot of fun matching wits with the bad guys who would and could have fed me to the sharks off Isla Mujeres had they known my identity and motives. The Bank had loaned just under a million dollars to Pedro Cantara Vasquez to purchase the 65' Hatteras documented under the name *Costa Brava*. Pedro was a Colombian national and a 10 year resident of Miami (of course with his Green Card), who owned a business importing cut flowers from Ecuador and Columbia. He apparently had sold a lot of flowers to have acquired an exquisite penthouse on Brickell Avenue, a couple of Mercedes cars for him and his wife along with a number of other toys including the Costa Brava.

His wife, Juanita Beltran de Vasquez was a graceful woman in her late forties who clearly enjoyed the elegant lifestyle of the United States over her previous existence as a struggling model in her native Bogotá. Contrary to her late husband's love of boats she was frequently sea sick, hated the sea, the Hatteras and boating in general, unless of course, the boat might be the Carnival cruise ship *Fantasy*. When we first met I was interested in the circumstances surrounding the day when she had found that the Costa Brava was missing. She said that she hadn't been to the marina for at least three months before Pedro had died then added, "I think it may have been two weeks or so after poor Pedro went to heaven that Carlos called me, Carlos works at the marina and is also from Columbia so we became friends. When Carlos called he didn't know of Pedro's sudden passing as he had been on holiday. Carlos told me that when he had returned from his holiday he noticed the Costa Brava wasn't in its slip and thought Pedro was maybe in Bimini fishing." My first step was to contact the manager of the marina office who had no record of the vessel checking out. I found that after Pedro died someone had paid two months dockage, in advance. The marina's copy of the receipt had no name and was made out to cash. I then went over to the security office to see what they might know. Before I could barely get the words Costa Brava out of my mouth, Irma a sleazy blonde in a black Mickey Mouse look-a-like uniform, blurted out, "they don't know *nutin* about the boat and didn't *saw* it leave." Who are *they* I asked. With obvious sarcasm Irma said *they* were the other guards that worked at the marina and she was sure no one had seen the boat leave. It hadn't been reported as missing and as the dockage had been paid, no one was concerned. I established that Irma and two other guards worked most nights and three others did the day shift and swing. In speaking with the other guards I learned that when a boat leaves there generally isn't a formal record kept unless the vessel may be one that's behind on their dockage fees, but this would be unusual as this up-scale marina rarely had deadbeats to contend with. In leaving the security office one of the guards named Peter pulled me aside and quietly suggested I meet him after his shift ended at Chuck's Steak House a restaurant favored by the boat crowd located on 17th Street in Ft. Lauderdale. Peter was a savvy, street wise type who was of the opinion that he deserved much more recognition than he received as a low paid security guard.

His first question was, "how much is the reward for getting the boat back?" Back from where? Do you know where the boat is? I told Peter that my client hadn't authorized me to offer any reward, but if he had facts that may be helpful in the investigation and the ultimate recovery of the Hatteras, I'd be prepared to personally pay him for any specific information that may be useful. He insisted that I keep his involvement secret and anything that I paid him must be in cash. I agreed saying, "Tell me what you know and I'll tell you what it's worth." Peter said that about a week after Pedro Vasquez had died he saw Don Francisco Marquez sitting with Irma in a green Jaguar in the owners' parking lot just before her shift started. He hadn't thought too much about it until two days later when he saw them meeting again in the parking lot, but this time he saw the Marquez give Irma a large brown envelop. When Irma opened the envelop he saw her pull out a neatly wrapped stack of money. Peter said he knew the Mexican, Don Francisco Marquez because when Carlos Vasquez was alive Marquez was a frequent visitor to the Hatteras. A few days after he had seen Irma with Marquez a third time, Peter said the Costa Brava wasn't in her slip. When Peter mentioned to Irma that the Hatteras was gone, she had told him that if he knew what was good for him, he'd better keep his mouth shut. I told Peter that I didn't know exactly what Irma's meeting with Marquez may have to do with the Hatteras, but as a gesture of good faith I'd pay him $500.00 for the information. I said that if I was able to establish a connection between Irma, Marquez and the Hatteras and we got the boat back I'd give him another $1,500.00. He gave me his home telephone number and address in Dania and we agreed that he would let me know if he came across any further information. A week later Peter called to tell me that he had a friend who was working on the fuel dock and had some information that may be of interest, His friend told him that when he had topped off the fuel tanks of the Hatteras there had been three very nervous Mexican guys on board. The fuel dock attendant, a Cuban, knew they were Mexican from their accent and when they paid for the fuel they also had some Mexican Pesos mixed in with the U.S. Dollars. With a full 1,800 gallon capacity the fuel on board would be sufficient for the Hatteras to easily make the Marina Hemmingway or Varadero on Cuba's north coast, refuel and then proceed to one of the Mexican ports of either Progresso in the northern Yucatan, Cancun or Isla de Cozumel.

I had some reliable contacts in Havana and another in Progresso, Mexico and asked them to check the marinas to see if there were any 65' Hatteras' which may have recently arrived. The inquiries proved negative. I didn't have a secure informant in Cancun and because Vasquez and Marquez had according to Mrs. Vasquez done some fishing in Cancun I decided to check this harbor personally. If the boat wasn't there I'd then move on to the other Mexican ports where the Hatteras might be and check them out personally. I started with Cancun arriving on the afternoon American flight from Miami. After picking up a Volkswagen Beetle from AVIS I checked in at the Fiesta Americana and went down to Friday's for a Cuba Libre. Cancun in the Mexican State of Quintana Roo is a narrow peninsula with a large protected lagoon on one side and the Caribbean Sea on the other. Most of the larger boats generally are moored in marinas on the Caribbean side along the Blvd. Kukulkan. With a miniature camera, digital recorder and three bottles of Evian I headed south on Kukulan stopping at a number of marinas before arriving at Carlos & Charlie's Dock. Passing the restaurant I made my way to the outer dock. In looking eastward toward the Caribbean I found a 65' Hatteras flying a Mexican flag; it had no name on the transom or on the topsides. I walked past the Hatteras slowly moving down the dock to a 1970's vintage Bertram 31' stopping briefly to admire this classic beauty. With the Hatteras now at a 45° angle to my left I could see that the forward hatches were closed, the sliding door from the cockpit to the main saloon was shut and the air conditioning pumps either weren't working or the a/c wasn't turned on. In the 90 degree heat with the door and hatches closed and no a/c running it was a pretty good bet that no one was on board. I returned to the stern of the Hatteras casually looking over the boat while taking a number of photographs with my camera held covertly in the palm of my hand. I focused on the hull identification number (HIN) visible on the starboard side trying to convince myself that with 20/20 vision I should be able to read the numbers, but other than HAT the manufacturer's identification code, the remaining nine numbers were blurred. At three in the afternoon the pier was empty except for a young lad who was concentrating on some varnish work at the end of the dock and a half dozen people in the restaurant chatting over a local cerveza.

I tried to convince myself that I could easily jump the few feet to the dive platform and take a rubbing of the HIN and be back on the dock before anyone was the wiser. The people in the restaurant appeared to be Yankee-doodle tourists, but what if they weren't or a restaurant worker or waitress saw me? I had to have a rubbing of the HIN to positively determine if this Hatteras was in fact the Costa Brava. If it was the Costa Brava and I got caught going on board without permission I could easily be arrested or even worse fall into the water, in any event my cover would be blown; the boat would probably disappear again and we might never get her back. I pondered my options and decided to wait. I got back in my Avis Beetle and drove down the road to the Cancun Marine Club, drank a bottle of the Evian then returned to Carlos & Charlie's, parking between a swarm of other Beetles where I could watch any activity on the Hatteras. At about five the restaurant was empty and there was still no activity on board the Hatteras. During the time I had the Hatteras under surveillance I compared the photos I had been given by Mrs. Vasquez with the Hatteras I was watching. The gold outriggers were a match, the ships bell in the cockpit to port was a match and my unnamed Hatteras in Cancun had a life raft secured on the foredeck with a blue cover next to a dinghy winch to port which also matched the Costa Brava. I casually strolled into Carlos & Charlie's and ordered a Coke. The waitress, a Canadian, was friendly and asked if I liked Cancun. I said that I was a little bored with the beach and wanted to go fishing, inquiring if any of the boats in the marina were available for charter. She said that the Pescador (the 31' Bertam I had admired) and the big boat at the end of the dock which only arrived recently in Cancun was taking half and full day charters. I returned to the Beetle and continued working on my notes. A little after six a red Volkswagen station wagon pulled in and parked next to the restaurant, the two male occupants got out and made their way to the Hatteras. The two stayed on board for about 30 minutes then moved to the restaurant where by the greeting they received from another waitress, they appeared to be regular customers. An hour later they left, with me following a safe distance behind. I followed until they left the peninsula and drove toward the old city located on the mainland. For future reference Í made a note of the poorly lit dock at Carlos & Charlie's which partially obscured the view of the Hatteras at night noting also that the dinner crowd doesn't' normally start to appear until after nine.

I returned to Carlos & Charlie's Dock a bit after ten, first checking if the Red VW station-wagon was there, then checking the bar to see if the two Mexicans had returned by other means before meandering down to the Hatteras. Between ten and midnight the restaurant was buzzing with a few couples strolling hand-in-hand down the dock after dinner. From the restaurant the Hatteras was partially obscured in the shadows of the marina dock that was deserted. With only a few sheets of paper torn from my notepad and a soft pencil I dropped to the dive platform of the Hatteras and in a few seconds had a rubbing of the HIN from the transom. On the drive back to the Fiesta Americana I compared the HIN from the Costa Brava to the one from the Cancun Hatteras—they matched—I'd found the Costa Brava. Now, how do I get it back? I called my clients to give them the news and they too asked, how do we get it back? I briefly explained that we'd probably have to do a snatch and grab. While enthusiastic in being able to recover the Hatteras they made it very clear that they would not condone any illegal activities, but were interested in how much it would cost and if the Hatteras be recovered without exposing her to any danger. I ended the conversation with assurances that I'd get back to them.

This was a job for the Clan and needed military precision if it's to be carried out successfully. The following morning I called New York to present my proposal; I felt that if I could recruit them, this was a job for the Clan. With the payment to the three South Africans (the Clan), my fees and expenses, fuel and dockage costs we could put everything together for about $30,000.00. The only potential danger would be if the Mexican Navy was able to stop the Hatteras before it could leave Mexican territorial waters. They would arrest the Clan and return the Costa Brava to Cancun. If this happened I wasn't sure how I'd get the Clan out of the slammer, but the Hatteras wouldn't be any worse off than it was before. The client agreed it was worth a try and would provide the funding, but made it clear that they would deny any knowledge of the exercise if it failed. I requested certified copies of the U.S. Coast Guard documentation and the loan agreement. A few days later FedEx delivered the vessel's documentation papers and $30,000.00 was wired to my bank. My contact in Progresso had confirmed that Marquez was not only a very bad guy, but that he also had the police authorities in Quintana Roo on his payroll. This clearly meant that I couldn't approach Mexican law enforcement in seeking their assistance in recovering the stolen boat and if Marquez had any inkling that we were on to him he'd remove both the hull identification numbers on the boat and the Hatteras could again disappear. To get the Costa Brava back it would have to be *Here Today & Gone Tomorrow*.

I left Cancun the next day and returned to Puerto Rico. The snatch and grab of the Costa Brava would have to be well planned, quickly executed and above all that no one would get hurt—or killed. The Clan would be a perfect match; I needed at least three persons, two men and a woman to do the deed. The three of them could do the job while appearing like tourists when they chartered the boat. The woman would drive the Hatteras while the men took care of the two Mexican crewmen. The Mexican Navy has a base at Isla Mujeres and a gaggle of run-down patrol boats providing coastal surveillance between Cabo Catouche and Punto Allen. They kept a Frigate in the port of Progresso which was normally out-of-service for repairs. During the time I had lived on the island of Sint Maarten in the

Netherlands Antilles I had made a number of friends and having spent a number of years in Durban and Johannesburg was particularly drawn to the South African sailors who had made this Dutch island their home. They were generally experienced, big, trustworthy specimens of mankind who possessed a special knowledge of the sea, but who also enjoyed a cold beer equally with making money. Two hours after arriving in Philipsburg I had located the Clan and explained the mission pointing out that if it failed they could end up in a Mexican jail. The Clan included Pieter, his wife Fran and Jacob, Fran's brother. They agreed to carry out the *snatch-and-grab* of the Costa Brava in return for the sum of $5,000.00 each. The plan: I would purchase a small 9' inflatable boat from Wal-Mart and a chart of the Yucatan peninsula south to the Guatemalan border. The Clan would purchase round-trip tickets from Sint Maarten to San Juan. I would purchase the Clan's round trip air tickets from San Juan to Mexico and make their hotel reservations through a local travel agent. The following Saturday the Clan would fly from Sint Maarten to San Juan where I would meet them. I would provide them with three business class tickets on COPA's afternoon flight from San Juan to Mexico City via Panama and $900.00 in cash. The tickets would be round trip so as to avoid any possible problems with the Mexican immigration authorities that could arise if they only had one-way tickets. Pieter, Fran and Jacob were to play the roles of tourists on their way to a holiday in Cancun, just like millions of others before them. When the Clan left Mexico it would not be by plane. The Clan would each carry only one small sports bag only. The COPA flight was scheduled to arrive in Mexico City at 10:57PM. The Clan would have reservations for two rooms, in their names at the Mexico City Marriott Airport hotel.

From the airport in Mexico City the Marriott is accessed over a walkway, if the plane was on time they would be in their rooms by 11:45PM. The next day they would have reservations on the morning Mexicana Airlines flight to Cancun. Upon arrival in Cancun the Clan would take a taxi to the Cancun Hilton and await my call. I made it clear that no one in Sint Maarten is to know of the Clan's travels and no phone calls are to be made from the hotel room's phone in Mexico City or Cancun. I arrived in Cancun on Monday afternoon and checked into the Fiesta Americana; from a pay phone I called the Hilton. Fran answered the phone and I told her to take a taxi to Carlos & Charlie's Dock and make a reservation to charter the Hatteras for a full days fishing on Wednesday. They should then take another taxi to the Calinda Hotel. Next to the Calinda is a small bar called the La Bodega, I would be waiting. The La Bodega is popular with tourists which would allow us to blend in without drawing any unnecessary attention. I wanted all of the Clan present to insure everyone knew exactly what was coming down. We'd have one chance to pull this off—there was zero tolerance for error. Before meeting with the Clan I would go to Carlos & Charlie's and book a half-day charter on the Hatteras for Tuesday afternoon. The name I used for the charter was Thomas A. Chance, a tourist from San Francisco. I paid them the $550.00 half-day charter fee in cash. When they asked where I was staying I said Dos Marinas Condominium, I said that I was staying with a friend who owned one of the condos. In case they asked, I was ready with the number of an empty unit, but they didn't ask which one. T.A. Chance got his receipt and left. When asked later why I used the name I said that I felt T.A.C. was appropriate considering I was clearly Taking A Chance. Her Caterpillar engines had been recently serviced and the Costa Brava had been hauled, anti-fouled and had her zinc's replaced two months before Vasquez had passed away. I had obtained an inventory list of what was on the vessel before Marquez stole her from Miami but needed to check to see during the charter what equipment was working and how much fuel was on board. The Costa Brava had been equipped with all the vital components such as a 72NM radar, SSB and VHF radios, two video depth sounders, EPIRB and a Robertson autopilot, hopefully it all was still working.

I didn't know what charts were actually on board the Hatteras so I picked up a copy of the Reed's Nautical Almanac for the Caribbean and a chart of the Yucatan coast. The Clan would have the chart of the area and the Reed's Almanac which they could use for the harbor areas. I knew the Clan would manage. My charter of the Hatteras was uneventful; the Mexican crew was pleasant and accommodating. While on the bridge after departing Carlos & Charlie's Dock I was able to confirm that both engines and the main Kohler generator were running fine. According to the engine synchronizers the engines were humming along at 2200 RPMs with a clean bottom we were making just over 30 knots. The propellers and shafts were running smoothly with no vibration. All the electronics were functioning and the radar set at a range of 16NM, told us we had a clear path ahead. While one of the crew was at the helm on the flying bridge the other was in the cockpit setting up the fishing gear and preparing the bait. The main VHF radio was not turned on. I casually asked if the radio worked at which time the helmsman turned it on quickly adjusting the squelch that pierced our ear drums. Turning it off he said that they never turned it on because of the constant and boring chatter. The Hatteras had tanks that held 1,800 gallons fuel, the gauges indicated that the tanks were 3/4 full—we had at least 1,350 gallons. Of the 445 gallons of fresh water we had at least half on board. About five miles out I got into the fishing chair and played the role of the novice angler for about an hour catching a few small Dorado before complaining of seasickness. I said I didn't feel well and wished to return to the harbor. Having been paid for a half day the Mexicans had no problem returning the *gringo* to the marina. I then made my way to the La Bodega and waited for the Clan in a corner booth. I briefed them on the day's events reporting the fuel and water levels, the condition of the engines and generator, oil and transmission pressures and the electronics. The only thing I didn't know was exactly how much if any, extra oil was on board. When we had returned to Carlos & Charlie's Dock the engine room door from the cockpit was open and I saw two five gallon pails of Texaco URSA engine oil, but had no idea how much was in the pails. At 8:00am on Wednesday the clan would check out settling their hotel bill in cash and take a taxi to Carlos & Charlie's Dock.

The plan was for the Clan to carry their three small/soft sports bags in which they would have the tightly wrapped Wal-Mart children's two-person inflatable, a roll of Duct Tape, 12 MREs (meals-ready-to-eat) which I had obtained from the U.S. Navy Base in Puerto Rico, a current chart of the Yucatan coast, and the Reeds Nautical Almanac, all of which would be covered with their clothing. After leaving the dock Fran and Jacob would go up on the flying bridge to engage the helmsman in conversation, Pieter would remain in the cockpit with the other crewman. Once the Hatteras was offshore about six to seven miles, Jacob would give a nod to Pieter at which time they would grab the diminutive Mexicans forcing them to the deck. Fran would move the throttles to idle (about 900 RPMs) and place the transmissions in neutral. While Jacob held the helmsman down, Fran using the duct tape would secure his wrists behind his back then move to the cockpit to do the same with the crewman being held by Pieter. Acting simultaneously with the element of surprise the Mexican crew should be overcome quickly and without any injuries. Once the helmsman has been taken from the bridge to the cockpit both Mexicans are to have their ankles securely wrapped in duct tape in addition to a single wrap around their mouths and eyes. It is important that you move quickly to prevent the crew from grabbing one of the fillet knives in the cockpit or the flare gun secured in a locker on the bridge. Once the Mexican's had been overcome and were secure, the Clan would not speak but communicate only by hand signals. After the Mexican crew had been securely *wrapped for shipping* the small rubber boat would be inflated. After it was inflated the Mexicans would be taken to the dive platform and gently put into the rubber boat back-to-back making every effort to keep water out of the little boat. Taking the flare gun and six flares from the Hatteras which will be secured in a Zip-Loc bag and four bottles of drinking water would be placed between them in the center of the boat. Both of the Mexican's understand English and therefore the only time anything is to be said is after they are placed in the rubber boat. Fran should then explain to them in English that they should take care in moving around in the rubber boat because as well as drinking water there's a flare gun placed between them that could go off.

Fran should then tell them that if they capsize the boat they will lose the flare gun and may become shark bait. When the rubber inflatable is cast off Pieter should spin the little boat to disorientate its occupants. When the Hatteras moves away and being disorientated the Mexicans can only guess what direction it may have taken, but they will most likely opt for the closest landfall which would be a northeasterly course towards Cuba and the Florida Keys. While Pieter drives the Hatteras on a southeasterly course Jacob and Fran are to do a thorough inspection of the boat's vital systems. Jacob is to inspect the bilge's and insure all the pumps are working, go through the engine room to check the Racor fuel filters, belts, stuffing boxes, shafts, seals, through-hull valves, hoses and connections. Fran is to literally tear the boat apart making a complete and thorough inspection of the interior, checking carefully for drugs, narcotics and firearms. Firearms are to be thrown over the side. Anything else that can't be identified or looks suspicious is to be wrapped, secured with fishing hooks and weights and thrown overboard. The Mexicans in the inflatable boat will most likely be spotted by other vessels transiting the area as the north setting current moves them inshore towards Puerto Juarez. In any case it shouldn't take the Mexicans much time to loosen the duct tape once they figure how to put their hands overboard into the sea without capsizing the boat and begin firing the flares. My little Mexican friends might be uncomfortable for a few hours, but would have a great story to tell the senoritas. Once the little rubber boat had been set adrift and the Hatteras had moved to a point at least a mile from where they had cast off the Mexicans, Pieter is to turn on the ship's VHF radio, switch to channel 71 and in his best Spanish transmit two words, *ADIOS AMIGO*. I will monitor channel 71 on my hand-held VHF radio and upon receipt of the signal from the Hatteras will respond, *Si Senor*. A few minutes after 10:00AM the Hatteras sent its *goodbye friend* and I replied *Yes Mister*. The Hatteras was on her way. To avoid possible detection a Mexican naval patrol boat who may get their position from Doppler radar, radio silence was to be strictly maintained until the Hatteras entered the territorial waters of Belize. They would however keep the channel scan activated to see if there was any radio traffic about their dirty deed as they fled the scene.

Once outside of Mexican jurisdiction and with her US documentation on board the Costa Brava if necessary could use her radios. I determined that the closest safe refuge would be Belize City, some 250 nautical miles to the southwest of Cancun. If the Hatteras ran at about 2,200 RPMs she would make a speed of about 33 knots completing the passage in just over 7.5 hours. On Tuesday when I had chartered the boat she had about 1,350 gallons of fuel on board with say a 10% reserve, this would provide at least 1,215 gallons of useable fuel. If my calculations were correct and depending on the sea state the engines would burn between 92.4 and 99.0 gallons per hour at 2,200 RPMs. To make the trip on a worst case scenario of burning 99.0 gallons per hour we'd need 742.5 gallons of fuel. If the Hatteras needed lube oil I prayed that the five gallon pails I'd seen in the engine room were full. I also hoped the fuel was clean, but if not that there were spare fuel filters on board. With the Hatteras on its way I checked out of my hotel and headed for the airport. I was a able to catch an AeroMexico flight to Mexico City that connected with a flight to San Pedro Sula in Honduras and then make the short hop to Belize City. At dusk I arrived at the airport outside Belize City and took a cab to the Radisson Fort George Hotel & Marina. Even though I knew it was much to early I still looked out over the Caribbean Sea in anticipation of seeing the lights of the Costa Brava approaching in the distance. The next morning I went down to the marina to arrange a berth for the Hatteras and to check with the authorities. Just after 11:00am I saw that my ship was coming in. Pieter had arrived off Caye Caulker in the early morning hours and even though he had the Reed's Almanac to use as a pilot, wisely decided to wait until dawn before weaving through the outer reefs and making his entrance to Belize City. After securing the Hatteras in the marina and clearing in I invited the Clan to lunch. The MREs had kept them going on the trip down but Pieter, Fran and Jacob were ready for a real meal. Over lunch they recounted the last 24 hours which they said had been fairly uneventful. Pieter said that the two Mexicans virtually wet their pants when they were overcome and made no effort to resist. No doubt a sound decision considering the 250lb muscular builds of the two former rugby Springboks. Fran had added a personal touch when she told the Mexicans that if she saw them move too soon she'd turn around and run over them with the Hatteras. That hadn't been in the Plan, but what the hell!

The Clan confirmed that the Mexicans sat frozen still as long as they could see them in the binoculars. About two hours out they lost the port engine due to a clogged filter, but were able to change the filter and restart the engine in about 10 minutes. They maintained running at around 2,000 RPMs for most of the trip and said the seas were calm which made for a smooth ride.

◆   ◆   ◆

The snatch & grab of the Costa Brava had been carefully planned and executed with great professionalism thanks to the Clan. After securing the Hatteras and enjoying a good night's sleep I put the Clan on the morning American Airlines flight from Belize City to Miami connecting to Sint Maarten. Through the marina I arranged a caretaker for the Hatteras and paid two months dockage. I reported back to my clients in New York that the Costa Brava was safe and sound at the Radisson in Belize City. The clients were happy that she was being looked after by a responsible gentleman with whom I would check with on a regular basis. The bank who held the paper on the Hatteras worked out an arrangement with the widow for them to take possession of the boat so it could be sold. Mrs. Vasquez was quite pleased as she never really wanted the Costa Brava in the first place. Working through the bank I met with an interested party who subsequently purchased the boat to use in a fishing business in the Cayman Islands. After deducting the recovery costs the widow received a payment representing her late husband's equity in the boat. The bank recovered the outstanding balance of its loan plus the accrued interest. The Cayman Islands Corporation that purchased the Hatteras changed her name and reflagged the boat on the Cayman Registry. On her trip from Belize City George Town the newly renamed and reflagged Hatteras did **not** pass through Cancun.

The Wet Dream
Location of the Investigation: Dominican Republic and the Netherlands

I first met Jacob over an enjoyable dinner at the Renaissance hotel in St. John's, Antigua. Jacob, an experienced Dutch marine surveyor is employed by a reputable firm based in Amsterdam who on occasion traveled to the Caribbean on behalf of Dutch yacht builders. We had both come to the island Antigua to conduct a joint survey of a Swedish yacht that had been upgraded and refitted by a large yacht builder in Holland. Jacob was there on behalf of the builder, I was representing the Swedish owner who had several complaints with deficiencies that he wanted the builder to correct. Over the years I have had the pleasure to be instructed by members of the HISWA, the Dutch acronym for the Holland Yachting Group which includes such names as Jongert, Royal Huisman, Amels, Feadship and other premier manufacturers of luxury yachts. Sometimes I will represent the HISWA companies, other times, as in this case, I'll represent an unhappy owner. Early the next morning we drove to Falmouth where we met the yacht's captain who took us out to the boat which was lying at anchor. Jacob, being an engaging professional allowed us, without too much wrangling to agree on what was needed to be done to correct the deficiencies, and who would pay for it. Over dinner that night we finished off our business of the day when Jacob asked if I might be able to help with another, unrelated case. He said that in the late 1980's a large sailing yacht had gone aground on the north coast of the Dominican Republic and subsequently had been declared a CTL. He said, the wreck had later been purchased by a German who shipped her to northern Europe to restore it. It seems that following the alleged restoration which took a number of years, he had insured the vessel for €9,090,909.00 (euros). Jacob asked if I might know something of this vessel and its history before it was shipped from the Caribbean. I told Jacob that not only did I know the story of this yacht I had monitored its progress after it had been salvaged and was placed in the small shipyard in Puerto Plata. Jacob's mouth dropped open asking, "are you sure it's the same boat?"

I told him that I had been in Puerto Plata shortly after the yacht had run aground and because its hull was virtually destroyed and the fact it had been declared a constructive total loss by London insurers, couldn't understand why anyone would go to the expense of putting the wreck in the little shipyard. My curiosity was further aroused when a few months later I flew to Puerto Plata on another case; in visiting the shipyard I was surprised to find that the Wet Dream was still there and in even worse condition having been further ravaged by the weather and further looting. I was particularly interested in having a closer look at the condition of her sandwich construction and how it had withstood the initial grounding and subsequent exposure to the elements. The hull was made up of outer and inner laminates with a Divinicell core laid between the fiberglass laminates. The outer and inner laminates had separated from the Divinicell core which looked pretty grim from being exposed to grease, oil and the other excrement found in the waters near Puerto Plata. Over the course of the next couple of years during frequent return visits to Puerto Plata, Sosua and Samana and simply for academic reasons, I had made follow-up inspections of the wreck. I was interested in what, if any ultra-violet or mold damage was being sustained by the exposed Divinicell blocks as well as the development and advancement of corrosion of her internal metal components. The rudder blade had been knocked off, the keel and a large portion of the bottom of the yacht was missing. The keel remained on the bottom outside the harbor entrance where she had first struck the reef. There was a large hole on the port side. The delamination and separation of the core material from the laminates went from what remained of the bottom all the way to the deck/hull join. The Wet Dream had run aground at the entrance to the harbor of Puerto Plata on January 5, 1987, the salvage effort was lead by Joseph Erisman of Erisman Ship & Salvage Co. Immediately after the grounding on the evening of January 5, 1987, local residents (looters) boarded the vessel and in spite of the crew's efforts to stop them, began stripping the vessel's interior removing the gear and equipment through the large hole in the port hull. The local detachment of the Dominican Navy also had used the hull as a small arms target.

Underwriters had little option but to declare the vessel a constructive total loss. Believing that he might recover some of his costs Mr. Erisman purchased the wreck for $1,000.00 and had it transported to the small shipyard in Puerto Plata. After hearing my story, Jacob then tells me his story.

Apparently in early 1990 a German bought the wreck of the Wet Dream and shipped it to his company's yard (incidentally he wasn't in the boat business). The new owner of the wreck claims that over a ten year period he reportedly rebuilt the vessel, with amongst other little goodies like adding gold water faucets. Thanks to an accommodating marine surveyor who no doubt received a substantial fee, on December 20, 1999 placed a value on the vessel of €9,983.164.75 (euros). In addition to the surveyor having limited experience with fiberglass yachts of any size particularly large ones (he worked mainly on small wood fishing boats) he held no credentials whatsoever in yacht or ship valuation. In spite of the surveyor failing to inspect or note a totally delaminated hull that could not be repaired by the new owner, with this clearly self-serving survey in hand the German owner was able to obtain €9,090,909.00 in insurance on the vessel which at the prevailing exchange rate at the time was in the region of US$9,000.000.00. This amount of insurance would seem a bit rich considering that when the boat was under construction between the years 1981 through 1984; her new build cost was under US$1,500,000.00, which was the amount for which she was insured in London. Even if her hull had not been totally delaminated and even if she did have 24k gold faucets, this would have no bearing on the fair market value of a wrecked 1980s yacht whose hull had been totally delaminated and destroyed that it couldn't be repaired. What's also a bit strange is that this obliging surveyor then reviews and updates his December 20th 1999 *valuation survey* and in a single page letter dated January 20, 2000 the accommodating surveyor without any justification or reasonable explanation reduces his first €9,983.164.75 value on the vessel to €9,090,909.00. (Maybe the faucets were plated, not 24k?) On February 14, 2000 exactly twenty-four days after the insured value of €9,090,909.00 was accepted and confirmed by underwriters the vessel was totally destroyed by fire.

◆   ◆   ◆

Well as you might guess the European underwriters were more than a bit interested when Jacob reported back to them that I was not only familiar with the background surrounding the Wet Dream, but had actually inspected the wreck and had recorded the total delamination of the vessel's hull.

The total delamination of the hull would have prevented it from being repaired at least if they wanted it to float. During my various inspections I further noted that the 50mm x 50mm Divinicell blocks had obviously not been successfully adhered to one another during the hull manufacturing process. It appears that to reduce costs rather than using uncut sheets for the sandwich core, individual blocks were applied that required individual adhesion to one another. With few compound curves on a large hull the use of regular uncut sheets of core material would have been preferable, but would have somewhat increased the costs. I also found that a number of areas on the fiberglass hull displayed large areas of osmosis damage. Due to the depth and width of penetration of the outer skin the osmosis damage could not have been repaired. Underwriters were also interested in how the vessel's original insured value in 1987 could have increased seven fold over its new build cost. As you might guess the €10,000,000.00 or so claim filed by the German as a result of the fire is being disputed by the underwriters and is presently in litigation. There were other interesting aspects to the case in that the literature and brochures indicated the vessel was over 92' whereas her Cayman Islands registration documents showed her measured length was only slightly over 75'. Inquiries with the Lloyd's Register found they had no record of the vessel or the company that was alleged to have built her. Independent inquiries in Fort Lauderdale and West Palm Beach Florida, where she had been fitted out, concerning the vessel or her builders also proved negative. The underwriters were rightly concerned as to how a 1980s vintage wreck which hasn't floated on water since 1987 could be worth €9,090,909. It couldn't. The salvers who carried out the work, took possession and who actually owned the wreck at the time, pretty well described its condition in a letter to London solicitors dated May 24, 1988, "It appears that the continued deterioration of the vessel has made economic repair impossible and we are about to attempt to recover part of our costs by breaking up the hull and selling some of the usable equipment. The case continues, but much like they say in the opera it's not over until the fat lady sings, which also applies when it comes to insurance claims. It is indeed not over until the fat lady sings and in the case of the Wet Dream, the fat lady hasn't even come on stage yet.

Good News and Bad News
Location of the Investigation: Germany, The Dominican Republic and Florida

Hans Dieter was in his mid forties, nice looking and like most con artists a friendly, likable and a smooth, believable crook. He had come to Florida in search of his fortune and found it. Hans had entered the United States on a B-1 visa which gave him 90 days to enjoy Florida's hospitable climate as a tourist, but strictly prohibited him from working. During his first month he incorporated the Keys Construction Company of Miami, rented a Jaguar XJ and started frequenting the bars and restaurants favored by upscale Europeans. He shortly met a middle aged German lady who soon suggested he move into her luxurious town house in trendy Coral Gables. To avoid having to give out his lady friends phone and address he organized a mail service and got two cellular phones, one for his business the other for monkey business. The stage was now set. In short order Hans had a company, a jazzy address where he lived rent free and was driving an expensive car all of which gave him credibility. Even though Keys Construction was a shell company without any assets or construction projects he was able to convince a number of trusting Europeans to buy stock and lend money to him. During a short period, during which time he extended his visitors visa, he was able to amass almost $900,000. Ponzi conspiracies are a type of pyramid scheme named after Charles Ponzi an Italian immigrant who, back in the 1920s duped thousands of New England residents into investing their money in a scheme that involved speculation in postage stamps. Ponzi worked on the premise that he could take advantage of the difference between U.S. and foreign currencies used to buy and sell international mail coupons. His pitch was that he could guarantee them a 40% return in 90 days or less which compared favorably with bank rates of about 5% at the time. Ponzi found it hard to keep up with the money that was pouring in and reportedly took in over $1 million during one three hour period and this was in 1921! To make the scheme look legitimate Ponzi made sure a few early investors were paid off, but most lost their life savings. Ponzi schemes continue to work today on the principle of rob-Peter-to-pay-Paul.

Hans had created an illegal Ponzi scheme and you may wonder what this has to do with marine insurance, but please read on. During Hans's accumulation of wealth on the backs of others he met and befriended a German gentleman from Hamburg who happened to own an aging 65' Hatteras Sport Fishing boat that had a value of about $400.000. Gerhard (Gerd) Schroder was a shrewd business man who, while he was in Hamburg had made a fortune in the textile industry; he had retired and then moved to Florida. After meeting at a German watering hole in Fort Lauderdale and learning of his wealth, Hans hit on him like Bomber Command hit Dresden during WWII. Gerd liked Hans but couldn't be convinced to invest in Key Construction so Hans took another tack. The two met a number of times and casually spoke about taking the Hatteras to the Dominican Republic and setting up a sport fishing enterprise at the upscale resort of Casa de Campo. Hans convinced Gerd that he had extensive experience with operating a large boat (even though he didn't know one end from the other) and would be willing to move to the Dominican Republic, captain the boat, promote the fishing business and carry out the maintenance required. Even though Gerd had made millions in Germany and was unquestionably an astute businessman, Hans not only convinced him to become his partner in the Dominican sport fishing business, but do so with Gerd's own boat and his money. Because his visitors Visa had already expired and as a result of the September 11th Hans figured that his request for the renewal of his visitors visa by the Immigration and Naturalization Service would fall on deaf ears, he clearly risked being deported. Now was the time for Hans Dieter to relocate—outside of the United States. Other than simply being a smooth talking con man it's still not clear how Hans pulled it off but he got Gerd to give him a $400,000 Hatteras on a personal note of $150,000 and then obtain a bundle of cash to start a new business in the Dominican Republic. Even though the Hatteras was documented with Gerhard Schroder as the beneficial owner, Hans was soon on his way south to the Dominican Republic with the boat. Life in this third-world country began well for Hans. He hired a local crew to take care of the boat in anticipation of throngs of enthusiastic fishermen from the Casa de Campo resort who would be booking the boat for $850.00 a day fishing excursions. He rented a grand house overlooking the Caribbean and filled his days and nights boozing with a steady stream of young prostitutes.

Six months into the project Gerd began asking about his percentage of the income from the numerous fishing trips that Hans reported were being booked each week. Even though Hans had left Florida he was still being pestered with a number of lawsuits from disgruntled investors who he had involved in Key Construction. To protect his remaining assets he had secreted his money in a bank in the Bahamas before leaving for the Dominican Republic. Because the boat wasn't being chartered, Hans had no income and was forced into making increased withdrawals from his Bahamas bank account to maintain his lifestyle, pay the upkeep and dockage charges and the salary of the full time crew working on the Hatteras. After Gerd had turned over the boat to Hans he had formed a shell company in the Bahamas naming the Bahamian company as the owner of the Hatteras, the Bahamian company then gave Hans the Power of Attorney. Through a Canadian insurance broker he was able to over insure the Hatteras for $750,000 but for private and pleasure use only. He had not indicated to the insurers that the vessel was to be used for charter, with a paid crew thus avoiding the increased premium that he would be required to pay. Hans also conveniently didn't mention that Gerhard Schroder was the legal owner and that he, Hans Dieter had no insurable interest in the Hatteras. Running low on money that would most assuredly compromise his lifestyle, Hans decided to fake a $50,000 theft of fishing gear from the boat. As part of his scheme he reported the theft to the Dominican authorities and then filed an insurance claim. Normally when dealing with a marine claim I will first call the assured to schedule a convenient time to meet. However, in theft cases the claim is handled a bit differently. Before arranging to meet an assured I like to first visit the vessel to see where the vessel is kept, the general state of her maintenance and if I can see from the dock if there are any visible signs of forced entry. I generally don't know the assureds or anything about them nor do I know their financial situation. This information can be obtained later if needed. However, in many cases those who file theft claims do so to upgrade old equipment to state-of-the-art gear and equipment or because they are simply short of money. This has been in greater evidence due to the world financial climate following 9/11. I located the Hatteras at a small fishing club in an estuary near the Casa de Campo resort. I casually strolled down the dock glancing at various other yachts as I moved towards the Hatteras. Stopping at the stern of the Hatteras I asked the mate if the vessel was available for charter he said yes, half-day for US$500.00 or US850.00 for full day.

The mate invited me onboard and pointed out the expensive Penn reels, offshore fishing gear and other high value items needed and used by the aficionados of the sport, all of which I noted were on the theft report and on the detailed list of stolen items provided by Hans. Knowing that a Browning dive compressor and the Nikon underwater camera had been included in the list of stolen property, I said that my friends were also avid divers and if they happen to have a compressor on board and maybe an underwater camera. I was shown the Browning compressor and Nikon underwater camera that had been reported as stolen. I was also covertly able to photograph the equipment, the boat and her crew. Taking a few copies of the brochures offering charter services I departed. I called Hans a couple of days later arranging to meet him at a well known cafe in La Romana the following Friday. In the interim I prepared a letter addressed to underwriters detailing the policy information, the reported theft and Hans's withdrawal of the claim. In my meeting with Hans he said he was pleased that I had responded and how soon could he expect to receive a check in settlement of his claim. I told him I have been invited on board the Hatteras and found all the gear and equipment that he falsely had reported stolen; continuing I said, "Hans, I've got good news and bad news, what do you want first? With a puzzled look on his face he responded, "I don't exactly know what you mean, but please give me the good news first." I smiled and said, "Well Hans. The good news is that you've committed insurance fraud which you may know is a felony, but you may not have to go to jail" He turned a pale white as the blood rushed from his face and said, "What's the bad news?" "You're not going to be paid anything because nothing has been stolen. You are using the Hatteras as a charter boat when your insurance application states the use is private and pleasure only. The insurers may immediately cancel your policy and as we are now in the Atlantic hurricane season, that's not good." He asked what he should do. I placed the claim withdrawal letter before him suggested he carefully read it and sign it. I said I would fax his signed withdrawal of the claim to his insurers and in the meantime he should get religious. I suggested that he should pray that underwriters don't prosecute him and that they don't report the filing of a false and fraudulent theft with the Dominican naval authorities as being jailed in the Dominican Republic is a fate worse than death. He couldn't sign the document fast enough.

Upon my return to Puerto Rico I faxed my report which noted the excessive hull value, commercial use as a charter boat and the claim withdrawal document to the underwriters. This case was closed or so I thought. Six months later I found that the underwriters had initially canceled the policy, but reinstated it a short time later when I was instructed to deal with the Total Loss of the Hatteras which had been insured again this time for $750,000. Hans had somehow been able to return to Miami, so much for Homeland Security, and one way or another had conned the same underwriter to insure the Hatteras again. This was really a stupid move. Gerd Schroder after finding that Hans and the Hatteras were back in Florida got a judge to have the Feds arrest and detain the vessel. Having done a little research with some well placed friends in Miami I learned that Hans had been present when the vessel was seized and knew it had been returned to the rightful owner. He knew the Hatteras wasn't a Total Loss but thought he'd take another stab at his insurers, this time for $750,000. I called Hans in Miami and arranged to meet the following day; he was not a happy camper to learn that his friend from Puerto Rico would be dealing with his new Total Loss claim. There was no claim as the Hatteras wasn't a total loss, but undamaged, safe and sound moored behind a house in Pompano. It was again, Good News—Bad News time.

◆   ◆   ◆

In applying some basic investigative skills the underwriters avoided a $50,000 theft claim and a $750,000 Total Loss claim. The real resolution will not come about until underwriters make premium income secondary to inflated hull values and pay closer attention to who their assureds are or as in this case when Hans Dieter moves to the mountains of southern Germany where there's no place to float a big boat.

Wild Willie
Location of the Investigation: Hong Kong, Singapore, California & Mexico

During a passage from the Far East supposedly to Fort Lauderdale, Florida, a large custom built motor sailor reportedly sank some 500 miles south of Acapulco, Mexico. European underwriters concerned with the loss were asked to pay the policy limits approaching one million U.S. Dollars to the American owner residing in Singapore. With nothing more than a strong suspicion I was instructed to conduct an investigation into the circumstance of the loss. Within four hours after receiving a copy of the file I was on a Mexicana flight to Acapulco accompanied by my son Jason. Inquiries at the Acapulco Yacht Club (AYC) where I was acquainted with the manager revealed that the yacht had indeed stopped at the AYC in its trip south. The Yacht Club Manager said that the yacht had sunk about ten days previously, south of the Gulf of Tehuantepec an area known for it's violent storms. While at the Acapulco Yacht Club I found that all the crew had left Mexico with the exception of the vessel's Chief Engineer, who we will call "Willie". My *amigos* and *amigas* at the AYC indicated that Willie said he had no money and was desperately seeking work. The area around the AYC, unlike the club itself is an area of cheap hotels, bodegas and cantinas, mostly establishments of ill repute. With a photograph of the crew provided from the underwriting file Jason and I set out to begin on a track crawl search of the areas drinking establishments in an effort to locate Willie. After visiting about 20 or 25 bars in the area, we lost count after the first 10; we entered a small cantina on the perimeter of the search area and found Willie nursing a warm cerveza. Grabbing two stools next to the target we sat down ordering two cokes and some *tapas* in Spanish then began conversing in English much like the millions of other North American tourists who visit Mexico each year. After ordering another cerveza and obviously starved for English conversation Willie turned to the newly arrived tourists and inquired if they were Americans or Canadians? I responded that we were Americans on a visit from the Eastern Caribbean.

Unknown to Willie, underwriters had provided me with a crew list with all their details and particulars. I had a complete file on Willie, but politely inquired if he too was a tourist. Willie said no he wasn't a tourist. I then asked what had brought him to Acapulco. "Oh we just sank a boat and I'm waiting to be paid by the owner." Hoping that my son had maintained his composure I turned to find him smiling at Willie's revelation while listening intently. Somewhat surprised myself I continued the conversation by asking "But why?" Calmly Willie responded, "To collect the insurance money. This American Guy who lives in Singapore bought the boat for about a quarter of a million US then took it to Hong Kong where he got a crooked surveyor to put a value on the thing for a million bucks. The plan was to sail the boat to somewhere remote along Mexico's west coast where the crew could scuttle her and safely get ashore. The Mexican coast off Puerto Angel was perfect. We pull the plug, row ashore, have a short but well paid vacation and the owner collects a million dollars. After he gives the surveyor his 10% cut and pays us he walks away from the deal with a cool $800,000.00—tax free." Feeling I was on a roll with this yet-to-be-convicted-felon went on to ask, "Willie I don't know much about boats, but how do you make a boat sink?" He casually replied, "She had two big diesels in her so I just cut the salt water cooling lines." "Did any one get hurt?" Willie responded, "Oh no we were only about a mile from the shore so after we piled our gear into the Whaler, we just motored to the beach. The water was flat calm". During the conversation I was recording all the information and making mental notes considering that the Notice of Loss had indicated that the yacht was 6 miles from the coast when it sank which would have placed the vessel in water with a depth of over 3000 feet. Willie then said, "You know if you're interested I could send you some photographs that I took when we sank her. It took about 3 hours for her to go down, so I've got some great photos". The criminal justice system has found a pattern where most criminals after they commit a crime, normally have a tendency to brag about their crimes to seemingly disinterested parties. Arsonists like to watch a building they have set ablaze while murderers frequently may attend the funeral of their victims. Willie, obviously quite pleased with himself and the successful sinking of the yacht offered me the photographs he'd taken, but couldn't have the photos processed as he was really tight on money. Asking why he was short of money, Willie said that the owner hadn't paid him because the damned insurance company was holding up paying the claim for some reason.

Smiling in agreement I politely responded, "Bloody insurance companies will cancel your policy in the blink of the eye if you don't pay your premium, but the moment you have a claim and want your money they sit on it," Willie jumped at the chance when I offered to have the photos processed. After taking Willie back to his $1 a day hotel he gave me three rolls of 36 exposure 35MM film. After expending almost $1,500.00 at the local One Hour Photo Lab—I knew I would only have access to the negatives once—we met again with Willie at the La Bodega. I gave Willie the negatives with one set of prints. As he showed me the photos, carefully explaining each one I noticed that in a number of the photos Willie had taken there was a fifth person on board the yacht after they had cleared out of San Diego with only four. Falsifying the yacht's immigration clearance document is a federal offence. There were also a number of boxes stowed on the aft deck. The 8x10 enlargements that I had made of the photos showed the external markings on the packing, it was clear that the boxes contained Doppler radars, high tech electronic and radio/navigation, equipment that had not been cleared out by U.S. Customs in San Diego. Willie volunteered that the fifth person shown in the photos had been a female named Terry. Terry was the girlfriend of a Mexican drug dealer who was a fugitive from justice. Terry had been arrested in San Diego on narcotics charges and was out on bail. Willie said that the captain of the yacht had agreed, for a fee, to smuggle Terry and the high tech gear to Acapulco. The equipment had been offloaded before the vessel sailed south to be sunk when it would ultimately be *sold to the insurance company*, as Willie so nicely put it. After returning to Puerto Rico I prepared a full report to underwriters. Underwriters asked if I thought I could locate the vessel in view of Willie's statement that they had been only a short distance from the shore, not 6 miles out. After determining the height of the mast in relation to the height of the dunes along the coast I was able to calculate the exact distance the vessel was from the shore. It was less than 1.25 miles from the beach. Being familiar with this coastline and the progressive water depths I was able to determine that the vessel was lying in approximately 180 feet of water. I returned to Puerto Angel the following week and with the use of a chartered local fishing boat and a recording side scan sonar that I had packed in my luggage for the return trip, the yacht was located and photographed.

Underwriters working with the authorities had provided hard evidence of insurance fraud with the intentional sinking of the yacht, the harboring and interstate transportation of a fugitive from justice and the illegal export and trafficking in electronic equipment subject to Customs oversight.

◆　　◆　　◆

An experienced marine underwriter became suspicious in reviewing the preliminary Notice of Loss of a yacht in a remote part of the world. He became even more suspicious after speaking with me and obtaining my professional opinion as an accredited ship & yacht appraiser, that the insured value of the yacht had been grossly inflated by an unqualified surveyor in Hong Kong. The documents were turned over to the authorities for prosecution. Willie, in his desire to tell someone about the crime became pivotal and provided not only a running dialog of the events, but over 100 supporting photographs. Later when asked by the US Attorney who prosecuted the case how he thought the photographs had come into the hands of the authorities Willie said that he had met this nice American guy and his son who offered to have the film developed for him because he was short of money; he believed that the photo lab in Acapulco saw the photos they had probably called the Mexican Federal Policia Judicial who must have turned the photos over to the US authorities. My involvement was never revealed. Investigative work always involves close attention to detail and considering the 20 or 25 visits to local bars, a great deal of leg work. Most experienced investigators can create the circumstances and conditions that appear to provide the luck that leads to successful results. But sometimes they experience a break in a case that provides exceptionally good luck by meeting up with targets the likes of Willie.

Going..

Going...

Going....

Gone....

Thanks Willie...

The Cay that wasn't there
Location of the Investigation: Dominican Republic

Upon receipt of a Notice of Loss from underwriters I was instructed to contact the assured to take the necessary statements and confirm the actual loss of the property. The assured had reported the loss of his yacht, dinghy/outboard and all personal effects in a remote area of the Dominican Republic on the island of Hispaniola. The following day I arranged to meet with the assured at which time the owner said that he and his son had been sailing along the North Coast of the Dominican Republic and just after sundown had decided to find a place to anchor for the night. He stated that his 30' Sloop had been anchored approximately 100' from a white sandy beach in the lee of a small Cay, and that he was so close to the Cay that when the moon came up later that evening it cast a shadow over the boat. He couldn't remember the name of the Cay and couldn't identify it on a chart, but did recall the name of the closest village. The anchor line parted at dawn the next day and before he could get the engine started the yacht had grounded in raging surf. After the vessel was aground they stepped off the boat, walked ashore and proceeded to the nearest village for help. At the first interview after approximately two hours the yacht owner completed and signed his statement, but not before I had asked whether he was certain of all the various details and facts such as the distances from the beach, the Cay, the raging surf and the shadow that was cast over the boat by the moon in the lee of the Cay. He said yes, that's exactly what happened. The assured stated that the dinghy and outboard engine and numerous other personal effects had been safely locked in the cabin of the vessel before he left the area. When he returned everything had been stolen. During the first and subsequent interviews held with the assured he asked repeatedly, "Does that sound all right to you? Does it sound logical to you that it happened that way? Followed by, "Do insurance companies always conduct such a thorough investigation of such a small loss?" The claim amounted to just under $40,000. Unfortunately for the assured I am intimately familiar with the coast of the Dominican Republic and have friends who are commercial vessel operators, members of the Dominican

Coast Guard, a number of Port Captains including command rank Naval officers in the Capital.

Being aware that there are no Cays in the area that match the description where the vessel was reported to have stranded, the investigation began in earnest. There are two Cays on the North Coast of the Dominican Republic that remotely fit the description provided by the assured, one is 10 miles from the other and neither have a water depth that would allow anchoring. Also both Cays are downwind from the beach where the remains of the vessel were eventually found. The beach described by the assured was found with wave action of no more than 12" due to its sheltered position. After meeting with the local Port Captain in Samana it was discovered that the vessel was nowhere near where it was first reported to have grounded, and that all offers of assistance to tow the vessel into deeper water had been refused. When the Port Captain first saw the yacht it had not been washed up on the beach and was not hard aground, but only lightly touching the sandy bottom. The alleged stolen dinghy, outboard engine and personal effects had been given away by the assured. Sworn affidavits were obtained from all the witnesses and the recipients of the dinghy, outboard and personal effects who said that the assured had told them, "The insurance company would pay for everything." The assured promptly retained a Criminal Lawyer, most likely as he considered the possibility of underwriters prosecuting him for insurance fraud, however after realizing that a strong case had been developed proving he had lied, the claim was immediately withdrawn.

◆   ◆   ◆

Working together as a team the in-house claims handlers kept in close contact with the yachts owner and during the investigative process maintained a close control of the flow of documentation to and from the assured. With a sound knowledge of the coast of the Dominican Republic I was able to determine that the description of the loss provided by the assured was inconsistent with water depths, location of Cays and beaches.

The observation was also made that under normal circumstances a free floating yacht will move with the prevailing currents and winds, not against these forces. In concert with local Law Enforcement contacts, the investigation was able to produce leads to eyewitnesses, location of the stolen gear and sworn affidavits from all those involved that could be used in the event the underwriters wished to prosecute. The underwriters Special Investigations Unit provided oversight coordination that brought everything together for an airtight case of blatant marine insurance fraud. However, as the assured assumed that he may be prosecuted for insurance fraud he wisely withdrew his claim. In reflecting on this claim it appeared that the assured simply may have made an honest mistake in his navigation along the Dominican Coast and had gone aground. Insurance covers stupid decisions and errors in navigational judgment, as long as they are not premeditated. In the event of a fortuitous loss which in plain English means accidental that gives rise to a claim, it's **always** advisable to tell the truth. Many people seem to believe that if they hit a reef because they didn't look at the chart they must make up a story to tell their insurance carriers 'to make it sound good.' This is wrong and if the adjuster is trained and doing his job, he'll know it's a cock-and-bull-story and will catch you. Even if your story of the loss makes you look stupid, that's what insurance is for. In always telling the truth of what happened the adjuster can then effectively guide you through the recovery process, get your boat repaired and see that you receive the full benefits provided by your policy. The insurance company normally wants to keep you as a client, that is unless you've got a claims record that exceeds the national debt. In keeping you as a policyholder they want you to have your boat repaired as soon as possible at the best possible price and they want the boat returned to you in the condition it was before the loss—that means in a safe and seaworthy condition. Any adjuster worth his salt will do his best to help you through the claims process. Don't ever lie, don't create a story. Every lie requires another lie. Insurance fraud is a felony. Don't do it and you won't have the worry of getting caught.

Where's the beef?
Location of the Investigation: Dominican Republic, Haiti, Jamaica

A 3000 gross ton refrigerated ship sailed on the tide from Santo Domingo bound for the port of Miami to load meat products bound for Port au Prince, Haiti. For reasons yet to be known the ship's crew, rather than being signed on by the Master of the ship, had been signed on by the ship's agent in the Dominican Republic the previous week. The 25 year old ship had just come out of dry dock at 1700 hours on the day she sailed. She had also just been subjected to a full survey that rendered her safe, sound and seaworthy for her intended use. At 0800 hours the following day I received a call from the vessel's hull underwriters indicating that the ship was aground near the Haitian border where she reportedly had struck a reef. Before leaving the office to deal with the loss I contacted a local towing company in Santo Domingo and asked them to mobilize their 6000 horsepower tug and proceed to the stranded vessel. Following their arrival in this remote area it was clear that all communications would have to be carried out by means of VHF radio over a predetermined channel. Six hours later I had arrived at the scene and waited on the beach. Two hours after I had arrived I made a VHF radio call to the Tug as she approached the stranded ship. The ship was lying approximately 500 yards offshore in the pounding surf solidly wedged between coral heads in no more than 15 feet of water. The ship had an in ballast or unloaded draft of 16 feet. I met with the Tug's master and the salvage master appointed to refloat the vessel. A plan was agreed that incorporated the use of 350 pound ground tackle set in a Bimini pattern off the Tug's port and starboard stern secured to a large drum winch on the aft deck. Because of the low water depth the Tug had to remain just over 400 feet to seaward of the stranded vessel. While the lines were being secured and to await high water; using a small boat I boarded the stranded vessel. I first interviewed the Dominican crewman who had been steering the vessel and found he had previously never steered a ship of any kind, had never seen a nautical chart and in any case didn't know how to read one and didn't know how to operate or read the depth sounder even if it had been working. The helmsman also spoke only Spanish. The master of the Ship was a Jamaican who held a current Jamaican Home Trade Certificate of Competency, he spoke only English. The Masters on a small ship is the navigator because of the language problem he could not communicate with the Dominican charged with steering his ship.

At 1700 hours on the day of the incident after departing Santo Domingo, the Jamaican Master had merely pointed in the direction he wished the ship to go. At 2100 hours he again pointed in the direction he wished the ship to go, then went to bed. The Dominican helmsman continued in the direction the Master had pointed, until the ship impaled itself on the reef that was directly in the ships path. Further inspection found that the ship's sole binnacle compass had a glass covered top that was so discolored that you could not see the compass rose or any points of the compass. Even if the Dominican helmsman knew how to read a compass he could not have seen the points on the compass. In speaking with the Jamaican master I found that the surveyor who had recently completed a full inspection of the vessel rendering her safe and seaworthy had never looked at the compass. The compass hadn't been swung in 10 years and had no deviation card. The surveyor had not inspected the condition of the vessel's life rafts, which should have been condemned, failed to note faulty electrical wiring throughout the vessel, failed to note that the vessel carried insufficient personal floatation devices (life jackets), failed to note there were no pyrotechnics (flares) or signaling devices (large portable lights) nor that the vessel's radar was inoperative. The master of the vessel said he had noted all these deficiencies which were called to the attention of the ship's agent and the owner himself before they sailed from Santo Domingo. Getting back to the salvage effort, when the tide had risen to its mean height, the refloating of the vessel to deep water by a stern tow was commenced. In groundings such as the case at hand and to minimize further hull damage, the vessel would be moved slowly aft in the same direction that she had traveled in entering the reef. At this point the ships topsides above the waterline began to move while from the hull at the waterline remained wedged between the coral heads. Internal inspection of the hull shell plate revealed that the shell plate at the waterline had rusted so badly that the metal was literally paper-thin and as such was being separated and torn in two. By continuing to pull, the top of the ship above the waterline would sheer and be separated from hull below the waterline. It was then revealed that the "survey" had been limited to coffee on the bridge and had not included the vessel's gear and equipment or inspection of the hull which was now known to be totally wasted. The hull simply would not withstand the forces exerted by the tow.

Based on the manning deficiencies, the unsafe and improper condition of the ships electrical and inoperable radio/navigation equipment, and the total deterioration of the ships shell plate, the vessel was declared to have been unseaworthy at the commencement of the voyage and therefore in breach of the implied warranties of the policy. The Tug was released and the salvage abandoned.

◆   ◆   ◆

The claim was denied by underwriters and the ship remains as a derelict where she impacted the reef. Fortunately there was no loss of life and no cargo was sacrificed as she was not loaded and in ballast at the time of the stranding. Marine surveyors or adjusters charged with assisting in a salvage effort should first make every effort to insure against loss of life and minimizing loss to the property. In concert with these efforts they should also conduct a comprehensive on site investigation into the probable cause of the casualty and the general condition of the yacht or ship to determine the actual condition of the vessel, the condition immediately prior to the stranding and the condition at the commencement of the voyage. These important observations allow underwriters an opportunity to evaluate the claim and issue instructions to those on scene and how they are to proceed. While it may have some limited use, never rely on someone else's survey report.

The vessel remains on the reef—rusting away.

The Doctor's Dilemma
Location of the Investigation: Puerto Rico

A Physician resident in Texas kept his 46' sport fishing boat in Puerto Rico where he traveled twice a year for holidays. Underwriter's instructions requested an inspection of the damages sustained when their assured's boat allegedly struck a sand bar/reef and sustained "extensive damages to the hull, propellers, shafts and other underwater components." The report of the loss had been sent to underwriters allegedly only a few days after the damages had been incurred, yet the assured said he had already completed the repairs. The assured agreed to send the repair accounts to underwriters for settlement. He claimed that his broker had not advised him that a surveyor on behalf of underwriters would be required to confirm the damages before repairs were undertaken. The assured believed the process would be limited to sending in the repair bills and a check in settlement would be forthcoming. The faxed instructions were received during the evening hours the same day the loss was reported to the underwriters. At 0600 hours the following day, I visited the yard where the repairs were said to have been undertaken, but found no damage to the hull, propellers, struts or shafts. What I did find was a vessel in the final stages of extensive repairs to correct a serious Osmosis problem. Included in the documents provided by the assured were repair estimates from the yard to affect the repair of major hull damage to the keel and to port and starboard hull surfaces, renewals of (2) propellers, (2) shafts and on and on. Repair costs totaled over $ 10,000.00. A close inspection and a total of 36 photographs were taken of the vessel's hull and running gear to confirm that no damage had been sustained. The propellers, shafts and struts were not new nor had they been reconditioned. The yard refused to discuss their estimate of repairs. The vessel was quickly put back into the water and removed from the marina, but not before I had completed the early morning inspection and taken the photographs for evidence. It was apparent that the assured had purposely delayed reporting the loss believing that underwriters would not be able to confirm the damages or verify the cost of repairs. The assured had attempted to have the vessel's Osmosis problem and annual dry docking carried out at underwriter's expense. Underwriters chose not to prosecute the assured for his rendering a false notice of loss or his attempt to defraud his insurance company.

◆   ◆   ◆

Immediate and prompt response to any claim can sometimes be critical. The 0600 hours inspection revealed a blatant attempt at insurance fraud. Had I not carried out the inspection promptly the vessel would have been relaunched and underwriters presented with inflated and fraudulent accounts. The claim could have been denied but not without leaving underwriters exposed to spurious and costly litigation. By not reporting the loss until almost all of the work had been completed the assured had hoped to have all the work carried out before underwriters could effect an inspection. This clearly was a case of premeditated fraud.

The Flower Pot Caper
Location of the Investigation: Puerto Rico, Venezuela

While the owner of a large motor yacht was away on a hastily arranged business trip[1] his vessel unexpectedly sank at her slip. Instructions received from European Underwriters requested an investigation to determine, without prejudice, the cause of the sinking, resultant damages, related cost of repairs and the retrospective and current Fair Market Value of the vessel. In the early stages of the investigation underwriters modified their instructions to include and address the issue of mitigation of damages by the assured. It was reported that during repairs to the vessel's exhaust system two smooth sided flower pots had been used to plug the 12" port and starboard exhaust lines. The cause of the flooding of the machinery space was due to the dislodgment and movement of one or both of the flower pots placed in the exhaust lines. Smooth sided plastic flower pots, if used on board a yacht, are normally found on deck filled with plants or flowers, they are not generally used in the machinery spaces as watertight plugs. Neither of the flower pots had been secured with mechanical fastenings, but were simply forced into the exhaust hoses to stop sea water from entering the vessel while she was alongside the dock. In the inspection of the machinery spaces only one flower pot was found, the second pot was never located. Using the bar code label, which was still in place on the bottom of the remaining flower pot, inquiries found that the pot had been purchased at a local Wal-Mart Discount Store. Through the Bar Code it was found that this line of flower pots had been received into the stores inventory only 2 days before the sinking. The exhaust repairs were reported to have been underway for two weeks. With the loss of watertight integrity of the flower pots, located at the waterline, the vessel sank in a water depth of 12'. Two days after the sinking, the vessel was raised and refloated by salvers for a fixed price of $22,500.00. The additional damages estimated at $10,000, sustained during the salving effort were caused by the lack of rea-

---

1.   In contacting the airline the carrier confirmed that the owner's flight reservation had been made the day before the vessel sank.

sonable care by the salvers and is normally recoverable by the owner and/ or his underwriters under provisions defined as salvers negligence. After the refloating of the vessel the owner allegedly instructed a local shipyard to clean the vessel and pickle her machinery. These instructions were said to have been verbal, which is contrary to normal shipyard procedures.

Neither the owner nor the shipyard could provide the written record of the reported servicing instructions. A week following the raising of the vessel an inspection was carried out, which revealed that other than an external wash-down to remove surface mud, little or nothing had been done to mitigate the damages or preserve any of the vessel's machinery or operating components. The vessel's twin diesel engines and generator sets were found with surface rust and with internal components seized. At this time the owner then demanded that the twin engines and generator sets be renewed. Deteriorated interior furnishings and coverings had not been properly cleaned or given proper ventilation. The damages to the furniture and fixtures had been accelerated with extensive damage due to humidity and condensation.

ACQUISITION OF THE VESSEL

The agreement to purchase the motor yacht was executed in January of 1989. The hull was laid in February of 1989 with final construction and launching on 31 August 1989. In the owners application for insurance it was found that a number of material misrepresentations had been made including, but not limited to the altered year of build of the motor yacht. The year of the vessel was shown to be 1992 whereas the actual date of build had been 1989. It is important to note that a vessel's age is determined by the date the keel is laid—not the date the vessel is launched. In the United States, federal regulations require that all recreational vessels have a 12 digit HIN or Hull Identification Number permanently imbedded into the upper starboard side of the transom. The 12 digit HIN found on this particular motor yacht ended with B989 confirming a date of build of February 1989. From inception the owner of the motor yacht had experienced serious defects and deficiencies with the hull and machinery, defects and deficiencies that had lead surveyors to declare the vessel as being unsafe, unsound and unseaworthy. As early as 6 months after delivery to the owner, his surveyor rendered an opinion that the vessel should be confined to port due to the loss of structural integrity of the hull. The Italian builders ignored repeatedly requests from the owner to remedy the defects and deficiencies or give him another boat.

Since its mandated introduction on 1 November 1972 the HIN must include in its format, the U.S. Coast Guard assigned 3 digit (MIC code) Manufacturers Identification Number, a 5 digit production or serial number and an alphabetic letter for the month of build i.e. A for January, B February through L for December. The 10th numeric digit is the year of build with digits 11 and 12 representing the model year. Model years run from August to July of the next year. As an example, a vessel built in July of 1993 would, in the last four digits of the HIN, show G393. If the keel of the vessel had been laid in August, the last four digits would read H394 for a build date in August 1993, but a 1994 model year. It is a Federal offense and a felony for anyone to alter, mutilate or remove a vessel's HIN. Every vessel has a hidden HIN obtainable only from the manufacturer for use by law enforcement or insurance investigators working with the authority of underwriters at interest. The Federally mandated HIN enables a trained surveyor or investigator to determine the builder, production/serial number and age of any vessel built in North America or a foreign built hull destined for importation into the United States.

THE ISSUE OF VALUE

Under the Uniform Standards of Professional Appraisal Practice in appraising the subject property, two approaches are generally considered in determining the present and/or retrospective valuation of a vessel, Cost and Market, also referred to as the sales comparison approach. In applying the Cost approach methodology considerations such as physical, technological and functional obsolescence would be addressed in percentages of depreciation over the life of the subject vessel.

FAIR MARKET VALUE

The most probable price in cash or terms equivalent to cash, for which the appraised property, if exposed for a reasonable time, will sell in a competitive market under all conditions requisite to a fair sale, with the buyer and seller each acting prudently, knowledgeably, for self interest, and assuming neither is under duress. In the case of this 1989 motor yacht based on the original acquisition cost of $1,000,000.00, had the vessel been free of defect it could be reasonably expected that the vessel's normal depreciation would fall in the following range:

1st year ('90)	15%–20%	$150,000	$200,000=	$850,000 to $800,000	(net value)
2nd year ('91)	10%–12%	85,000	96,000=	765,000 to 704,000	(net value)
3rd year ('92)	3%–5%	22,950	35,200=	742,050 to 668,800	(net value)
4th year ('93)	3%	22,261	20,064=	719,789 to 648,736	(net value)
5th year ('94)	3%	21,593	19,462=	698,196 to 629,274	(net value)
6th year ('95)	3%	20,945	18,878=	677,251 to 610,396	(net value)
7th year ('96)	3%	20,317	18,311=	656,934 to 592,085	(net value)

During the perusal of prior reports of condition and valuation commissioned by the motor yacht's owner, opinions had been rendered by surveyors without credentials in yacht valuation that yacht values often increase with age. This assumption has no basis of fact and ignores the recognized standards of professional appraisal practices. With the possible exception of some cases of early classic yachts, or vessels such as STORMY WEATHER or SANTANA, once owned by famous luminaries such as the late Humphrey Bogart, or currency fluctuations, that may apply during contract negotiations, production vessels of this size and type do not increase in value. In fact, less than popular manufacturers and models often experience accelerated depreciation, that in view of Agreed Value policies often compromise underwriters' interests and those of involved lending institutions as vessels do not increase in value. During the 1980's Savings and Loan crisis in the United States, the Resolution Trust Corporation, an organization charged with the liquidation of grossly inflated marine loans, were hard pressed to dispose of these loans without substantial negative deficiencies. In early 1990 the owner of the motor yacht, after experiencing numerous problems, reported to the builders that the vessel was suffering from serious hull structural failures and other major defects with machinery. These discrepancies clearly indicated the sub-standard construction, unsound and unseaworthy condition of the vessel. The repeated complaints by the owner to the builders culminated and were summarized in various reports prepared by the owner's surveyors in which they included their observations further confirming the vessel's unseaworthiness. The builders failed to respond or meet their obligations under the hull warranty, claiming that the failures were a result of abuse by the owner.

Litigation was found to be arduous, with excessive costs and ultimately proved unsuccessful. Based on the analysis of the historical data and a personal inspection of the motor yacht, it would be viewed. From an appraisal perspective at the lowest level of value[2]. In support of this position one would include such factors as:

Excessive Functional Obsolescence: The design and utility of the motor yacht is no longer desirable or economical compared with current state-of-the-art replacement vessels.

Excessive Physical Obsolescence: The vessel is damaged or worn beyond repair where the cost-to-cure cannot be justified.

Excessive Economic Obsolescence: External factors, such as market demand, severely limiting the potential sale of the vessel.

Considering the structural condition of the vessel during late 1990 and early 1991 her FAIR MARKET VALUE may well have been limited to the scrap value of her operating machinery and components and less than

---

2. Landesberg, Jack L., "The Lowest Level of Value", American Society of Appraisers, The Machinery & Technical Specialties Journal, Fall 1995

$250,000.00[3]. Under the General Conditions of all marine insurance policies, the burden of responsibility to maintain a vessel in a seaworthy condition rests solely with the assured. This is commonly referred to as the implied warranty of seaworthiness. 'Seaworthy' means fit for the vessel's intended purpose. Seaworthiness applies not only to the physical condition of the Hull, but to all its parts, equipment and gear and includes the responsibility of assigning adequate crew. For a vessel to be seaworthy, it and its crew must be reasonably proper and suitable for its intended use. Port Risk insurance: In principle, this is a time policy by which a ship is insured whilst she remains within the confines of a specified port area. In practice, an alternative form of port risks insurance allows the ship to navigate outside the port area. Prior to the assessment of the actual damages sustained and evaluation of sue & labor provisions in the mitigation of damages, it is important to first address the cause and effect of the sinking. It is a matter of record that the ingress of water to the vessel's interior was the result of the dislodgment and failure of an unsecured plastic flower pot[4], improperly placed in the opening of the exhaust lines which were located at the waterline. The owner was away and there was no Master and no caretaker present at the time the vessel sank.

Underwriters may view such behavior as willful misconduct of the assured resulting in a possible denial of all claims. Without proper sealing or plugging of the exhaust lines during repairs and the use of a plastic flower pot to maintain watertight integrity, seriously disregards the requirement of the owner to protect and maintain the vessel in a seaworthy condition. The responsibility to maintain the vessel in a seaworthy condition is required regardless of whether the vessel is allowed to navigate or subject to Port Risks Only. While the vessel is afloat, the Seaworthiness provision applies and cannot be ignored. It was a matter of record that the motor yacht was structurally unsound, unseaworthy and unsafe and the subject of unsuccessful litigation against the builders. In view of the prevailing circumstances it is apparent that the owner may have had little

---

3.   Based on a depreciation schedule of approximately 50% of replacement value
4.   The lack of hose clamps, mechanical fasteners/screws or waterproof tape

interest in keeping the vessel; because of these circumstances the *moral hazard*, the risk of a loss occurring by reason of intention or lack of responsibility of the assured cannot be ignored. Based on Bernoulli's equation for fluid mechanics found in a book on the same subject written by Victor Streeter in 1988, a 12" hole, similar to the exhaust line, with a I" head (the "head" being the vertical distance from the hole to the waterline) would provide an area of 113.10 square inches, permitting the inflow of 2828.9 GPM (gallons per minute) to enter a vessel's interior. This is based on one 12" hull penetration. If both exhaust lines were open the water flow would be doubled. The report of a rapid partial sinking of the motor yacht is consistent with the estimated water flow. The only factor preventing the total submersion of the vessel was the water depth of 12' of the marina and her being tied to the dock.

SUE & LABOR PROVISIONS

Upon the refloating of the vessel the assured was obligated to immediately take steps to mitigate[5] his damages. It would appear that with the exception of some initial pickling of the engines, minimal steps were taken to mitigate the damages or preserve the vessel's interior. Since the date of loss the vessel's interior furnishings and fittings sustained further damages and loss due to high humidity and condensation. The subsequent and secondary damages would not be covered under the policy. Various materials, which as part of the investigation had been removed from the motor yacht, were placed in sealed evidence bags and were submitted to an independent laboratory for testing.

The first Sample (A) was a foam material that had been installed on the vessel's cabin soles as a carpet backing. The second sample (B) was an overhead insulation material commonly used in yachts of this type. Sample (C) was a white oily substance found on the surfaces of the port generator control box (an area that was reportedly not subject to submersion). Laboratory tests of the three samples revealed a wide range of Elements including,

---

5.   Your Duties After Loss as referenced in all marine insurance policies

but not limited to, (CI) Chlorine, (AI) Aluminum, (K) Potassium, (Cu) Copper, (S) Sulfur and (C) Calcium. The lab results indicated that all samples contained elements of salt stating, "Semi-quantitative EDS analysis revealed all samples (A), (B) and (C) has been exposed to sea water. This information was significant considering the time period that had elapsed since the sinking and reported thorough cleaning and flushing of the vessel's interior. The normal steps that would have been required and undertaken by a prudent uninsured to preserve the condition of the vessel's internal components and machinery would commence immediately upon refloating, or during the salvage effort. Servicing of the vessel's main engines and auxiliary generators would take precedence over all other considerations irrespective of the weather conditions or the time of day. Even before the dry docking of the vessel, the mitigation of damages would be immediately undertaken by the owner, as mandated under the terms and conditions of the policy. Under all conditions the owner or assured must immediately take reasonable steps in mitigation of his damages as a prudent uninsured. While not limited to the following, it would be considered not only prudent, but mandatory to insure that the following procedures were undertaken to preserve and mitigate the damages sustained as a result of the sinking. The Sue & Labor provisions of Marine Insurance Policies provide for all reasonable costs and expenses to be for the account of Underwriters at Interest—free of deduction.

1. Pressure fresh water wash down of the entire engine room/machinery spaces

2. Removal of all external main engine components

3. Removal and pickling of all internal main engine and generator engine components. The ZF transmissions would be drained and pressure flushed with light oil before refilling.

4. The engine(s) would be continually turned and subjected to repeated oil and oil filter changes (minimum 4), until all traces of water had been removed. New drive belts will be installed.

5. During this process all engine(s) would be manually turned every hour. The injectors would be removed, cleaned and reinstalled following which the engine(s) would be started and run. The first running of the engine(s) would be for a period of 10 minutes followed by oil and filter changes. The second run would be for a period of 20 minutes minimum followed by oil and filter changes. The third run would be for a period of 1 hour followed by oil and filter changes. The fourth run would be for a period of not less than 2 hours followed by oil and filter changes. Lubricating oil samples would then be withdrawn for laboratory spectrochemical analysis. If the fuel supply was suspect, the machinery would be provided with fuel from portable containers.

6. In concert with the servicing of the vessel's machinery the related electrical components would be removed and replaced with new components. Treatment of all surfaces with Synco Super Lube© Teflon treatment, or a similar solution, would have eliminated rusting on previously untarnished/unrusted engine surfaces.

7. Pressure—fresh water wash down of the vessel's exterior

8. Fresh water hose wash down of the entire interior followed by cleaning with mild soapy water. All metal surfaces, door latches, hinges or other metal fittings should have been removed, cleaned and treated with Corrosion Block© or a similar preparation, which would have eliminated rust and corrosion on these now destroyed fittings.

9. All carpets, drapes and other furnishings would be removed for inspection. Those items that could be restored with dry cleaning or by other appropriate means would be so cleaned. The cost of any renewals would have been adjusted under the provisions of the Policy.

10. Following the fresh water wash down of all internal wood joinery the joinery would be cleaned with a mild soapy solution, hand dried and treated with Teak cleaner, brightener and dressing/sealer.

11. During the above preservation process the vessel's port lights would have been secured in the open position with a minimum of ten large oscillating fans placed throughout the vessel to insure the movement of air.

The foregoing mitigation of damages is, by their nature, labor intensive. The total number of man hours required would be viewed from two perspectives, labor and materials. Labor costs will vary depending on location and the level of technical expertise available. The first perspective being technical, would require the need of two experienced marine engineers providing approximately 60 man hours each at the rate of say, $50.00 per hour which would incur costs of some $6,000. The required parts and materials would be in the range of $4,000.00- to $5,000.00. Three unskilled laborers would be required for a total of 40 hours each for general cleaning and refinishing (120 man hours). Based on an unskilled hourly rate of $20.00 per hour, labor costs of $2,400.00 would be incurred. Had the owner observed the requirements of his policy to take all steps in the mitigation of damages, free of deduction, Underwriter's would have accepted the responsibility of these sue and labor expenses in the amount of $13,400.00 plus $22,500.00[6] for salvers charges and costs in mitigation of the damages. The final payment to salvers would have been adjusted depending on the success of recovery of claims dealing with the reported salvers negligence. In support of the accepted procedures and steps required to mitigate damages following a submersion, disinterested, but qualified, repairers were contacted who confirmed the recognized/ standard PICKLING PROCEDURES that should have been employed. Subsequent inspections of the motor yacht, a number of weeks after the incident, established that little, or minimal efforts had been expended to preserve the machinery and interior components or to mitigate the damages sustained as a result of the sinking.

_____

6.   Before adjustments for salvers negligence

MAIN ENGINES AND COMPONENTS

In contacting the engine manufacturers they provided vital information concerning the watertight integrity of their product in a cold submersion situation (a situation where the engines are not running and submersed to less than one atmosphere). The manufacturers provided specific details stating:

A. If the 1,500 horsepower diesel engines, such as those installed in the motor yacht are professionally cleaned and serviced following a cold submersion, these engines would not suffer any permanent damage and could, following replacement of any needed electrical components become fully operational[7].

B. The complete rebuild/reconditioning cost of this particular diesel engine is some $24,000.00. The new list cost of the turbo chargers is $4,165.00 each.

Had the vessel's main engines been properly and professionally serviced following the sinking, only minimal damage would have been sustained, damages that could have been economically repaired. Any subsequent claim for engine repairs and/or renewal, excluding those that would have been covered under the Sue and Labor provisions of the Policy, would not be for underwriters account. If technicians had indeed been instructed to pickle the machinery, and failed to carry out the required servicing, the cost of machinery renewal may best be directed to those responsible for post submersion care and maintenance. The engine manufacturer further confirmed that had the motor yacht sunk in 12' of salt water with an ambient temperature estimated at 700° to 800°, for a period of approximately 75 to 80 hours and if the standard procedures, as previously cited under items 1 through 11 were undertaken the engines would sustain minimal, if any damage whatsoever. The engine manufacturers stated that the

---

7. The engines of the motor yacht are sealed units. At the time of the sinking the vessel's exhaust lines were open thus allowing salt water to enter the engine(s) interior. Proper cleaning and oil treatment would have stabilized the internal components and prevented permanent damage.

turbo chargers would require cleaning, however due to their method of sealed construction the only part that may be required would be the renewal of the seal set. If however after running they emitted a white smoke the seals should be renewed. The cost of the rebuild kit per turbo, including all seals, is under $300.00. The cost per turbo of the mounting gasket set is $30.00. The list price of a new turbo charger is $4,165.00. The manufacturers added that the list price seldom applies for any replacement parts, as the discounts begin at 10%. As to the need to replace the alternator(s), in referencing the parts catalogue a list price of $4,100.00 is shown, however, if properly serviced, the alternators would not require renewal because of the ring seals that isolate the internal wiring from external case.

In pursing the possible need for replacement of the starter motors the manufacturer pointed out that the same watertight construction of the alternator is found on the starter motor, adding that the starter motor interlock is also protected by a watertight seal and under the description of the submersion in shallow water conditions it would not have been damaged. If the seal had been lost due to wear and tear then the new list price is under $200.00. Moving to the Glo Plug Controller, he stated that the control box should be inspected to insure no water had entered. The manufacturer pointed out that previous experience with submersions even in deep water for long periods of time, saw no water penetration. If the seal had been lost due to wear and tear this item could be renewed at a list price of $200.00. The manufacturer was adamant that no damage would be sustained if knowledgeable and experienced technicians had insured that all water was removed from the cylinders and the basic steps in the pickling process was carried out. These steps would insure that the engines would not suffer any permanent damage or loss of power.

INTERIOR FURNISHINGS. FIXTURES AND JOINERY

The interior wall covering was left unattended and eventually was damaged beyond repair, not as a result of the sinking, but due to the lack of prompt and proper cleaning. The resultant damage was caused as a result of humidity. The lack of initial cleaning, care and improper ventilation has damaged all hinges and other metal work beyond repair. The cost of these renewals and related costs are beyond the scope of cover afforded by the policy.

Salvage—Sue & Labor and Damages sustained as a result of the sinking

Actual Cost of Salvage: $22,500.00 + Sue and labor charges: $13,400.00 = $35.900.00 Excluding salvage and those items covered under the Sue & Labor provisions of the policy, replacement of those Items that may have been damaged as a result of the sinking totaled $ $108,230.00, including haul/launch and 90 lay-days. After a deductible of $20,000.00 the net repair costs for underwriters account would be $88,230.00. Whether or not the owner of the vessel was engaged in a criminal conspiracy rid himself of the vessel that had been defective from inception is unknown. What is known is that he attempted to fraudulently obtain $1,000,000.00 in insurance proceeds by having his underwriters declare the vessel a Constructive Total Loss will never be known.

The investigation into the claim revealed that material misrepresentations had been made by the owner that would have affected the decision of underwriters as to whether they would have declined acceptance of the risk. The renewal of the policy was undertaken by underwriters in good faith without being advised of the structural failures discovered or of the unseaworthiness of the vessel. The owner was privy to material information within six months of the first issue of the policy after his acceptance of the motor yacht from the builders. In addition to the fraudulent misrepresentation of the year of build, failure to advise underwriters of the major hull structural failures and resultant unseaworthiness, the motor yacht would have been over-insured virtually from the inception of the policy. With the exception of the defective part, damages resulting from latent defects are deemed recoverable under the 'Inchmaree Clause"; however, an assured who knowingly engages in material misrepresentations enables underwriters to void the policy from inception. Following a careful review of the investigation and the documented information surrounding the loss, the policy was rendered null and void. Insurance fraud is a felony in the United States. After considering the consequences of a criminal action, the assured quickly withdrew his claim. Underwriters closed their file without further need to pursue or discuss the issues concerning the mitigation of damages, sue and labor issues, or salvers claims. As the insurer is headquartered in Europe, the resources of the National Insurance Crime Bureau (NICB) could not be brought into play, nor could the case be recorded in their files. The NICB is a highly skilled organization that, working with law enforcement, investigates and maintains a record of criminal activities involving insurance fraud. The NICB database covers the entire range of insurance losses and claims including automobile theft, marine fraud and a host of others. This non-profit organization is funded by U.S. based insurance companies who have access to its services. As an overseas insurance company the activities and profile of the named assured could not be introduced into the NICB database to determine if he had previously engaged in the filing of questionable claims or introduce information to allow the creation of a record for future reference. Even though a complex case involving a number of elements, the successful combination and application of basic diagnostic engineering principles, a sound knowledge of marine insurance warranties and conditions, salvage and repair costs and basic principles of the valuation process, brought forth a truthful and fair resolution.

Maritime Security

Stowaways, Terrorists and other Perils of the Sea............

Webster's Dictionary describes a Stow' a-way' *n*. as one who hides aboard a ship, airplane, etc. to get free passage, evade port officials, etc. Over the years tales of the sea have depicted the *stowaway* as a colorful young character who seeks adventure by secreting himself aboard a tall ship bound for exotic locations where life can be sustained with ample quantities of coconuts and papaya which flourish in the warmth of a perpetual tropical sun. Through the pen of the likes of Robert Lewis Stevenson we are drawn to illusions of young lads who have slipped aboard majestic schooners of yesteryear only to be discovered a few days out by a warm hearted master who provide them with a berth in return for services as his cabin boy. In these fanciful situations the writers' imagination creates a colorful picture unrelated to the real life drama and fate of the true *stowaway*. Stepping back into reality ship security and in particular the stowaway problem is growing at an alarming rate and is not glamorous, but extremely dangerous. Today's stowaways can transport illegal narcotics, contaminated agricultural products and diseases. Ship owners and insurers alike are being faced with a problem that continues to grow and expand throughout the world with ever increasing costs. Political unrest and upheaval along with economic decline and decay in the Third World, are prime factors that motivate both men and women alike to seek the better life offered by the developed countries of North America and Europe. In 1996 the case of the MAERSK DUBAI graphically demonstrated the crisis and desperation of both stowaways and the ship's officers when uninvited Romanians were discovered after the ship had cast off from Algeciras in southern Spain. Bound for Halifax, the young Chinese Captain in being confronted with his unwanted human cargo took the inhuman step by casting them adrift in a makeshift raft where they later perished. As a ship is a rule bound domain governed exclusively and ultimately by her captain no one may challenge the order of the day as such actions may be deemed mutiny that offer severe consequences. While the Filipino crew was said to be appalled by such unmerciful treatment of the Romanian stowaways none dared to dispute the Captain's callous orders to cast them adrift in a raft of barrels and wood.

The Ship's Officers were brought before a Canadian Court under a charge of murder with the Filipino crew sworn to testify as witnesses for the prosecution. From 1991 to 1996 the number of recorded stowaway claims increased by over 400%. The cost of dealing with these claims by underwriters and ship owners has risen from some $350,000.00 in 1991 doubling to over $750,000.00 in 1995. In 1996 the number of incidents increased however, no doubt through gained expertise, the costs leveled somewhat at $725,000.00. Today the costs run in the millions of dollars. Other aspects of the stowaway problem we hear little about is health concerns and the transport of narcotics. Stowaways many times carry infectious diseases that without proper treatment can contaminate an entire ship or may even infect the port of arrival. Narcotics are the currency of the stowaway. Drugs sometimes purchased, many times stolen, are carried and used to barter when the illegals arrive at their destination. In analyzing the stowaway problem the word *reported* is a key word because there are many stowaway incidents where no reports would be made as the vessel's master or other officers are themselves involved in a remunerative stowaway conspiracy. And of course there are those stowaway cases that may not have been reported as they were dealt with as in the matter of the MS MAERSK DUBAI. The ports where incidents of stowaways are discovered are worldwide. Human cargoes secret themselves aboard ships in Puerto Plata and Santo Domingo in the Dominican Republic hoping to evade U.S. Customs and the Immigration Service in Miami or other US ports of destination. Men, women and children expose themselves to injury and death when they embark on illicit passages from the temperate zones of Africa and South America to the freezing temperatures of Canada and Northern Europe. Many times bodies are found in remote locations of a ship where without proper clothing, food or water the stowaways had perished during what they considered their trip to a new life. The cruel and inhumane case of the MAERSK DUBAI illustrates the drastic actions undertaken by a master to protect himself against the wrath of his owners. Owners and underwriters most assuredly would seriously question his competence and diligence in protecting the vessel against stowaways in a port such as Algeciras, known for its limited, if not poor security.

A ship's master who repeatedly transports stowaways is one that shore side management will view as irresponsible and unresponsive to the problem and therefore unworthy of promotion or advancement. However with a simple plan carefully employed, Masters can protect their vessels against unwanted incursion and the inevitable rage of their owners and insurers alike by taking a few simple preventative measures. In the first instance the ship's master and his officers should always consider every port as a potential danger zone; bearing in mind that the clever and determined stowaway is sometimes capable of evading even the most stringent security measures. However by employing comprehensive and consistent security measures the ship will become known as one that is difficult to obtain passage and the perpetrators will target other vessels with lax or no security. This is simply the path of least resistance principal. In view of the present and developing problems of vessel security, every ship must now have a designated safety officer who in some cases may also be charged with the responsibility as the vessel's security officer. The security officer is charged with the duty to insure that no unauthorized person or persons board the vessel while she is at anchor or in port. Initially it may not be practical to install video cameras that scan the decks of the ship while she's alongside or at anchor, but quite acceptable to have two members of the crew, for a modest additional consideration, designated as security watchmen. The ship's security officer after appropriate training would instruct his designated security watchmen in the basic principals of illegal entry and in concealment; the identification or areas of possible concealment and securing of these areas should be of primary importance. When discovered, physical contact with the illegals should be avoided and left to the proper port law enforcement authorities. The Second step in ship security is to evaluate the vessel for potential points of entry from the general arrangement plan. When at anchor or alongside the access is limited not only by the length of the ship but also something as obvious as the gangway. A recent case in Central America found that after a ship had weighted anchor and cleared the sea buoy a number of stowaways where found in the forward paint locker and another in the anchor well. In returning to port the authorities asked how they had come aboard, it was found that they simply used the gangway. The lesson learned, never leave the gangway unattended and always check any exterior openings, including the anchor well. One of the security watchmen should be assigned gangway duty when the ship arrives and during her stay.

If the security watchman must leave the gangway or there's is no need to have the gangway down after clearing and processing formalities, the gangway should be raised. Bulk carriers and general cargo vessels with low profiles and freeboards are easy targets. The Masters responsibility for the safety and security of his crew and ship is paramount. Since September 11th 2001 the rules governing maritime security have dramatically changed. The international maritime community which includes not only the full gamut of container ships, bulk carriers, oil tankers, LPG carriers and virtually any other ship that carries cargo, it also includes private yachts, mega yachts and any other vessel that carries passengers if they wish to remain in business, must comply with the Marine Transportation Security Act (MTSA) and the International Ship and Port Facility Security Code (ISPS) implemented by the International Maritime Organization (IMO). The Code requires that all vessels and port facilities that are involved in international trade, handle foreign flag vessels, dangerous cargo or passengers be in full compliance with the ISPS Code by July 1, 2004. The ISPS Code takes the approach that to guarantee the security of ships and port facilities it should be viewed as a risk management activity to determine what security measures are appropriate; an assessment of the risk should be undertaken in each particular case. The intent of the Code is to provide standardization and a consistent framework for evaluation of the inherent risks, enabling governments and local authorities to compensate and balance for variation in threat with changes in vulnerability for ships and port facilities. The process begins with each contracting government conducting port security assessments. There are three essential components of the security assessments: to identify and evaluate important assets and infrastructure which are critical to the port facility and clearly identify those areas and structures that, if damaged, could cause significant loss of life or damage to the port's economy and environment. This aspect of the assessment must clearly identify the actual threats to those critical assets and infrastructure and, in this assessment such threats must prioritize security measures and response.

And finally the assessment is required to address vulnerability of the port facilities by identifying the weaknesses in structural integrity, human security, electro/mechanical protection systems, security policy and procedures, communication systems, control and transportation infrastructure, utilities and specific high risk targets within the port's facilities. Not until the contracting government has completed a thorough assessment can they accurately evaluate and address the risk. The fundamental principle of risk management is embodied in the Code requiring a minimum of utilitarian and efficient security requirements for not only port facilities but also ships. In the case of port facilities the requirements include a port security plan, port security officers adequate for the facilities and a chief of port security. The security officers will also be required to be equipped with the specific gear and equipment needed to carryout their duties. In the case of commercial vessels they too will be required to have an appropriate security plan, a designated security officer from the ships crew in addition to a shore side company security officer. The ship is also required to have an appropriate inventory of security equipment to insure the safety of the ship. In addition to obvious gear such as hand-held radios this equipment may include firearms. Both port facilities and ships will also be required to have programs in place to monitor and control personnel and vehicular access and through 24/7 communications, the activities and movement of cargo and personnel. Of course, each ship or class of ship will present and require individual risk assessment. A container ship, car carrier or bulk carrier must have its risk factor assessed differently than a passenger ship, oil, product or LNG carrier. The method and procedures that they propose to meet and comply with the specific requirements of the Code will be determined and subsequently approved by the Administration or contracting government. To effectively make known and communicate a potential threat between a ship and a port facility the contracting government will establish applicable security levels. Such levels shall be Normal—Security Level (1), Medium—Security Level (2), and High Threat Conditions—Security Level (3). The notification of the security level would activate the appropriate security measures for both the ship and the port facility. (The full text of the ISPS Code is available from the International Maritime Organizations Website at www.imo.org)

Containers

The illegal entry problem is not restricted to ships but also include the containers that they sometimes carry. Because of the movement and location of containers that place them out of control of the ship it is virtually impossible to provide a simplified method of container inspection to guard against stowaways. Random inspection of seals and the use of a stethoscope to detect interior sounds, informants and a great deal of good luck may be the only way to determine that unpaid potential travelers are inside. I recently dealt with a case of a container that had been opened while in transit through the Caribbean enroute from Europe to the United States. The container had been opened and over $100,000.00 in liquor had been removed without breaking the seal on the right door. My investigation revealed that using a fork like pry bar, the center metal plate on the right door could be bent outwards only one inch which allowed the left door to be opened without breaking the seal on the right door. Once the liquor had been removed the thieves simply closed and relatched the door, then lightly hammered the center plate back into position; in applying a light coat of black grease over the plate the perpetrators effectively concealed the point of entry. The penetration of the container and theft went unnoticed by the shipper and the U.S. Customs Service (Homeland Security) during its movement from port to port until this 40' container reached the consignee and it was discovered that the contents had been pilfered. In this case the loss suffered by the cargo insurers was significant, but the real danger was what if after removing the liquor a terrorist had placed a dirty bomb inside the container to explode when it reached a U.S. port. This container was delivered to a port in the United States with its pilfered condition completely undetected by foreign and US authorities while it was in transit, and even after it had arrived in the United States. As part of the investigation I interviewed the security chief and management of this Caribbean trans-shipment port who were not aware of the thefts (I subsequently found that not one, but at least a dozen containers had been opened the same way) they believed their security procedures and their port facilities were totally secure. There is a serious lapse in security in many ports outside of the United States and Europe, ports that trans-ship containers between the U.S., Europe and the rest of the world. I can't say too much more of this particular case as it is now in the hands of Homeland Security.

Hopefully, law enforcement plugs this gapping hole in the security of containers before you read or hear on the evening news that terrorists placed a dirty bomb in a container that exploded in the port of Miami and killed or poisoned half the population of south Florida depending on which way the wind is blowing.

Cruise ship Security

While I don't think it's appropriate to call the original *Rainbow Warrior* a cruise ship, it was a high profile vessel known throughout the world as the flagship of the Greenpeace Organization. The tragic demise of the Rainbow Warrior nevertheless demonstrates the need for proper security and due diligence when faced with possible terrorist action. In February 1985 I had been instructed to conduct a condition survey on the vessel and was specifically asked to address the security of the ship due to the French government's displeasure with Greenpeace activities in opposition to France's nuclear programs in the South Pacific. After completing the survey I assembled the ships officers and crew, all of which were volunteers, to discuss the security issues. In the meeting I suggested various watch keeping standards and procedures, sensor activated deck lights, audio/visual alarms at points of entry onto the main deck, the bridge and the crew quarters. Considering the possibility of sabotage of the vessels propeller and shaft by divers I suggested to the master that the topsides be fitted with spotlights to illuminate the entire waterline of the vessel. Considering the possibility of underwater demolition, during daylight and the hours of darkness, watch keepers were to immediately sound the alarm if any bubbles were observed around the perimeter of the vessel. In spite of the surveillance procedures, divers of the French Navy and the French Security Forces were able to place explosives on the hull of the ship. The explosion caused the Rainbow Warrior to sink with the death of one person while alongside in Auckland, New Zealand on July 10th 1985. According to reports from Auckland City Police the Rainbow Warrior had been hosting a birthday party with 30 people on board when shortly before midnight two high explosive devices, which had been placed on the hull were detonated. The force of the explosions blew an eight foot hole below the waterline adjacent to the engine room. A crew member and the official Greenpeace photographer, Fernando Pereira, drowned while attempting to retrieve photographic equipment from his cabin.

The death of Mr. Pereira immediately turned the investigation from a terrorist attack into a homicide investigation. The small population of New Zealand was outraged and with extensive media coverage of the sinking it was soon evident that the French Security Forces were behind the bombing. Further inquiries lead the authorities to the abandoned Zodiac dinghy from the Rainbow Warrior and the French yacht Ouvea. The Ouvea had been chartered in Noumea and used to transport French agents and the explosives to New Zealand. The police soon zeroed in on a blue and white campervan and a French speaking couple; on July 15th Major Alain Mafart and Captain Dominique Prieur were arrested by New Zealand police. Mafart and Prieur were both identified as commissioned officers in the French Armed Forces who had been detailed to assist members of the French Security Forces to insure that the much publicized voyage of the Rainbow Warrior to Muroroa Atoll did not take place. Originally charged with murder, on November 4th Mafart and Prieur pleaded guilty to the lesser charge of manslaughter and arson. On November 22nd both were convicted each receiving sentences of seventeen years they were jailed in spite of intervention by the French government. The Rainbow Warrior was refloated and taken to the Devonport Naval Base in Auckland but following a close inspection Greenpeace determined that the damages were so extensive they reluctantly decided to scuttle the vessel.

The author and the *RAINBOW WARRIOR*

Over the last number of years I've had a unique opportunity to see first hand the workings, both good and bad, of a number of port operations in the Caribbean area. I've conducted loss prevention surveys on many types of vessels including port service vessels and vessels operated by the port authorities of Puerto Rico, Trinidad & Tobago, Curacao, Panama, the Dominican Republic and Jamaica. From what I've seen they all need urgent and immediate help. Cruise ship security in these and other ports present an entirely different set of problems and entirely different procedures to combat not only *stowaways* but the threat of terrorists. Maritime security has become the forte of the eminent Brigadier Brian Parritt CBE (RET) who, as the former boss of the British Army's Intelligence Corps soon became what is best described as the Guru concerning maritime security issues. The Brigadier has involved himself in advising passenger ship operators and ports on how to combat and defeat the 21st Century threat of terrorism at sea. Hopefully his clients believe in what he has to say and the world of shipping will be spared from another disaster. What may be viewed as a loss to Her Majesty's forces has become an immeasurable benefit to the worlds passenger fleets, ports and all those who go down to the sea in ships. For over fifty years the US Navy Base Roosevelt Roads near Ceiba, Puerto Rico has been contributing millions of dollars to the Puerto Rican economy in spite of negative and hostile actions by the local government. There are three political parties in Puerto Rico; the Popular Democratic Party or Populares, these are the ones in red that wish to continue with the commonwealth status, i.e. Washington keeps sending money to a Puerto Rico that doesn't want statehood or to be subject to U.S. taxes, even though U.S. taxes are less than those in Puerto Rico; they'd also have to give up the inhumane blood sport of cock fighting, The Greens or *Independendistas* would kick the United States out of Puerto Rico and create a new *third-world* country; the USA should disappear, but not their money.

The same group also emphasizes that Puerto Ricans would be prevented from speaking Spanish, as the English language would come with Statehood and may even be taught in the public schools. The Blue, New Progressive Party or statehood party believes that joining the Union is a good thing and supports the USA. The initial anti-American feelings were directly focused on the US Naval Base at Roosevelt Roads. The Base as it is known employed a few statesiders and hundreds of Puerto Rico's Red, Blue and Green residents; and since 1942 has supported America's Navy, Army, Marine Corps, Air Force, Coast Guard and in later years, Puerto Rico's Army and Air National Guard.

In providing services to the active military, the reserve forces and retirees, the Base had a modern marina and offered first class medical and dental facilities with one of the best Commissaries and Navy Exchanges south of Norfolk. The Base has been a blessing for the island of Puerto Rico and its inhabitants, who regardless of their party affiliation are all United States citizens that receive social security benefits, Medicare, unemployment and a host of other entitlements granted to the citizens of our great nation. Having spent sixteen years as a weekend warrior under the wing of the U.S. Coast Guard, founder of the U.S. Coast Guard Auxiliary in St. Thomas, U.S. Virgin Islands, Department Chief-U.S. Coast Guard Pan-American Auxiliary Liaison and a Merchant Marine officer, I was frequently on the Base. In support of our armed forces I became a director in charge of military liaison of the Eastern Puerto Rico Council of the Navy League of the United States (USNL) and subsequently was appointed Caribbean vice-president of the USNL which has its headquarters in Washington, D.C. On April 19, 1999 the tranquility of the Base changed when a Navy civilian contract employee working as a security guard at the Navy's training facilities on Vieques was accidentally killed during a navy training exercise. It was an unfortunate accident that crystallized the agenda of the *Independendistas* who kept pushing that Puerto Rico should be an independent country like its *third-world* neighbors the Dominican Republic and Haiti. One would feel that as these *Independendista* terrorists who all carry U.S. passports and enjoy the numerous benefits and entitlements they enjoy as American citizens would be in the minority. They are, but like many small radical groups they craved publicity and got it by destroying U.S. Government property, harassing the soldiers and sailors stationed on the Base and illegally trespassing through restricted areas. The *Independendistas* also harassed naval units from other countries such as the Royal Dutch Navy during exercises and attacked U.S. and German navy sailors on shore leave. Puerto Rico's less than illustrious Governor, Sila Calderon or as some have labeled her the self anointed *Queen* of Puerto Rico and her grunt the commissioner of police, instead of assuming a law and order stance and demanding that the Puerto Rican State Police uphold the law, they incited the Puerto Rican terrorists by encouraging violent demonstrations to oust the US Navy from Puerto Rico. This part Red/part Green *Queen* and her ignominious police ignored the repeated damage to U.S. Government property, injuries to U.S. servicemen, while vowing to kick the United States Navy out of Puerto Rico as part of her political agenda. The Calderon administration actively promoted an anti-American position and didn't stop the protesters from damaging U.S. Government property while she continued to request and receive financial handouts from Washington.

Of course it could have been a lot worse but for the fact that a large number of the Puerto Rico State Police had been indicted or were in jail on criminal charges ranging from narcotics trafficking, receiving stolen property and car theft. The banana republic mentality prevailed and escalated until the Navy temporarily stopped the training and the Base was subsequently closed. Why I mention this scenario, is that the Navy in an effort to stop the Puerto Rican terrorists from gaining access to the Base set up barricades with high caliber weapon fortifications and armed sentries at the entry gates, yet the harbor entrance remained wide open, especially on weekends and holidays (which are frequent in Puerto Rico) with a steady flow of recreational boats transiting the harbor. The MWR (Moral, Welfare and Recreation) Marina is situated close to the main docks of the Base that were frequented by Aegis guided missile destroyers, submarines, other surface combat vessels and warships of our NATO allies and were regularly alongside in the Surface Operations area near the MWR Marina. A number of the private boats in the marina and those that lie at anchor are owned by active duty, retired and others who can provide some reasonable explanation for being there. The marina also has a ramp where trailered boats can be launched; those who have access to the ramp only need to gain entry to the Base which only requires someone to sign them in. Trailered boats entering the Base are subject to inspection by Security, inspections which were rare or never done. I know because I spent six hours one weekend monitoring the movement of trailered boats entering the Base, not one was inspected. On one particular weekend during the summer of 2000 there were a dozen warships tied alongside including two submarines. This gathering of exposed warships would have provided terrorists with a potential Puerto Rican Pearl Harbor. I had gone to the MWR Marina for the inspection of a small sailboat when I noted a small motorboat being launched by a group that included two persons who I had seen in press photos taken of the demonstrators in Vieques. Considering the Fleet was in, I left the marina and drove towards the Naval Exchange where I stopped a security vehicle to report who I believed were anti-Navy protesters in the Marina. The two in the security vehicle said they'd look into it. As I left to return to the Marina I watched the Security vehicle drive towards the Mini Mart which is in the opposite direction of the marina. As the *Queen* has been successful in booting the US Navy out of Puerto Rico the problem no longer exists. On October 12, 2000 in the Yemeni port of Aden the USS Cole (DDG 67) was attacked by terrorists in a small boat laden with explosives. Unfortunately such attacks are destined to happen again. Commercial vessels provide the opportunity of a *soft target*, as demonstrated in the loss of the French ULCC (Ultra Large Crude Carrier) *LIMBURG* in the Gulf of Aden. These ships are ill prepared with minimal crews and lack the fire power to deter a determined suicide bomber intent on destroying himself and the ship he has targeted. Naval ships maintain a 24 hour watch to deter any vessel that approaches within the restricted area of 100 yards while underway or 200 yards when moored. Any small boat approaching within 500 yards of a military vessel is supposed to do so at the slowest safe speed. It doesn't take a rocket scientist to calculate the number of seconds it would take a small inflatable traveling at 50 miles per hour in a calm harbor, to cover 1,500 feet with 100 lb. of explosives and one terrorist hoping to meet in mortality the many virgins promised by bin Laden in reward for crippling or sinking a naval vessel or oil tanker. In the harbor of St. Thomas, U.S. Virgin Islands during the winter season sometimes four cruise ships carrying between 2,000 and 3,000 passengers each may be berthed alongside at the West Indian Company dock or in the anchorage both of which are a stones throw from the Yacht Haven Marina or the many yachts at anchor in the small harbor of Charlotte Amalie. Through the porous water border between Saint Martin/Sint Maarten, the British Virgin Islands and the U.S. Virgin Islands, penetrated frequently by drug smugglers and illegals, sufficient explosives could be obtained to kill or maim upwards of 12,000 persons simultaneously in one shot and would require minimal planning. Cruise ships lie alongside in Road Town, Tortola with no protection. The acting Commissioner of Police of the British Virgin Islands, who previously had a distinguished law enforcement career, most recently as Interpol's Head of Bureau in London, recognizes the potential danger that visiting cruise ships are exposed to, but hasn't the funding to do anything about increasing security. In Bridgetown, Barbados security is limited to disinterested cruise ship crews who roam the inner harbor in passenger launches looking for suspicious activity. During the winter season the cruise ships are generally coming alongside between the hours of 0700 and 0800. Normally the passengers are asked to return by 1700 hours in the afternoon. Waterside security is abysmal; a terrorist strike at 0730 or 1730 hours would insure maximum damage. There are large Muslim communities on all the islands, with countless bin Laden sympathizers. As an example in Trinidad it is not unusual to see pictures of Mr. bin Laden painted on the sides of business premises where, while not aggressively promoted, a subliminal anti-American bias is clearly evident. At a predetermined time either when the cruise ships first come alongside or during the late afternoon when the passengers return in anticipation of their departure a coordinated strike on three Caribbean islands could be executed. Six small explosive laden inflatable boats with 35 horsepower outboards positioned in St. Thomas, Tortola, BVI and Bridgetown Barbados striking at a pre-arranged hour, could sink or destroy a number of cruise ships within 15 minutes with major injuries and with a loss of life approaching or exceeding 10,000 people. Another soft target is the Panama Canal. Striking and closing the Panama Canal could be accomplished by a small explosive laden boat at either point of entry to the Canal at Balboa or Colon on the Caribbean side. An interesting aspect to the use of small recreational boats is that if the terrorist organizations were willing to spend a few dollars and didn't want to reduce the size of the organizations followers in suicide attacks, the boats could be easily fitted with small inexpensive auto-pilots. Once underway their explosive devices could be detonated by a cell phone. After September 11th we know that bin Laden's followers favored the use of airplanes to carry out their missions of death and destruction; most airports have at least some resemblance to basic security through the Transportation Security Agency (TSA). However, with thefts of passenger's personal items at TSA check-points numbering over 11,000 in 2003 and questionable pre-employment screening of the screeners the agency is clearly not as effective as we are lead to believe by the politicos. I once overheard a US Airways Captain define TSA as *Thousands Standing Around*. During 2003 a North Carolina college student demonstrated the efficiency and effectiveness of the TSA when he carried a number of nasty items on board an aircraft then sent the TSA an email advising of his penetration of their security. The TSA ignored the email and promptly filed it away. Little more need be said about the TSA except that it may help keep the unemployment rate down. In eastern Puerto Rico near the Navy Base the city of Fajardo boosts a nice airport where travelers can journey to the U.S. and British Virgin Islands; traveling from Fajardo also avoids the rather tedious drive to San Juan's airport. During November and December 2003 I used the airport a number of times as did countless others. The surprising thing about Fajardo's airport is that there is absolutely no security screening of passengers. If terrorists wished to destroy a cruise ship or two in St. Thomas or the British Virgin Islands and may suffer from seasickness, they wouldn't need a boat, but could conveniently carry out an attack using one of the multi-engine aircraft that fly in and out of Fajardo. One or two terrorists could simply pack a suitable quantity of C4 explosives, or in fact any explosive device that would detonate on impact and if they thought it was necessary, a small caliber weapon in their backpack and board one of the many flights that depart from Fajardo, Puerto Rico between 7:00 and 9:00am every day of the week. If our prospective bin Laden wannabe was a small terrorist, for weight and balance he would be placed in the co-pilot seat to the right of the pilot and have full access to the controls and instruments. Having most likely earned his pilot's license along with Mohammed Atta at any time during the 20 minute flight to St. Thomas, St. Croix or the other local islands, the terrorist could stick the weapon in the ear of the pilot blow him away and take over the aircraft. Once passed the Puerto Rican island of Culebra taking a course on the south side of the island, St. Thomas Air Traffic Control would no doubt attempt to contact the commandeered aircraft to determine its intentions. The impact of a twin engine Piper Aztec or B+N Islander might not have the killing power of an Airbus or 757, but would have an immediate and chilling effect that wouldn't exactly make the Virgin Islands or their visiting cruise ships the flavor of the month. In the case of the Panama Canal a determined terrorist organization could simultaneously sink ships at both ends of the Canal while at the same time strike and sink a laden boxship as it passed through the Miraflores Lock. The visitors parking area immediately alongside of the lock next to the old road between Colon and Panama City is less than 100' from the Miraflores Lock. The visitors parking area has been roped off due to the terrorist threat, however two terrorists sitting in the back of a small van equipped with RPGs (rocket propelled grenades) or shoulder fired stinger missiles (only two or three would do the job quite nicely) and easily sink any ship trapped in the confines of the lock. After firing the projectiles they'd simply close the sliding side doors and escape unnoticed in the confusion that would surely follow. RPGs and shoulder launched missiles are readily available from the Colombian ELN (National Liberation Army) rebels who are known to regularly cross Panama's penetrable southern border with Colombia. The dates and times of ship movements could be effortlessly obtained for a minimal payment to a needy employee of one of the many shipping company's in Colon or Panama City. If the strikes were carefully planned and coordinated for a specific type of ship or the specific time the ship was scheduled to pass, the Panama Canal would be closed indefinitely; east/west trade would immediately be crippled. If our terrorist(s) wanted to add a bit of drama when they closed the Panama Canal they could also add a bit of color for increased publicity and bring down the Pan-American bridge at Balboa. The northern span of the Pan American Bridge which links the South American portion of the Pan American Highway to Central America is supported by four, twin legged concrete pillars. The outer column is situated on a small island and accessible by a small boat. The next support column, some 500 yards to the north is on land. During the hours of darkness explosives set below the four concrete pillars of the outer and inner supports and detonated by remote control would collapse the Pan America Bridge into the entrance channel of the Panama Canal. The ensuing chaos with the collapse of the Pan American Bridget would further complicate shipping; and stop north and south bound road traffic for years to come.

The five easy steps for a terrorist to use an aircraft to attack a cruise ship in St. Thomas, U.S. Virgin Islands.

1. Depart from an airport that has no security screening and carry your weapon and explosives with you.

2. Take some extra explosives as checked baggage and go directly to the aircraft

3. Place the explosives in the cargo hold.

4. With St. Thomas on the horizon kill the pilot and take over the aircraft.

5. Crash the plane into one of the cruise ships moored in the harbor or alongside the West Indian Company Dock in St. Thomas, the flight takes 20 minutes from Puerto Rico.

Unfortunately Puerto Rico is not the only island in the Caribbean that has airports without passenger and baggage screening or proper security measures.

With easy access cruise ships present themselves as *soft-targets* to terrorists. Yachts are anchored in the harbor of St. Thomas only a few meters away from the cruise ships. Much like the USS Cole, a small boat could easily sink or seriously damage a cruise ship with little effort.

Three ships + one day = potentially 12,000 targets.

Terrorists have easy access to cruise ships by land or sea.

Small passenger ships with easy access also present *soft-targets* to enterprising terrorists.

Foreign flag yachts could easily be commandeered and used by terrorists as command centers.

The Central Intelligence Agency

CIA = Chaos-Ineptness-Arrogance

Those of us who are fortunate enough to make our homes in the West Indies, an area best described as the last paradise on earth, have heard and read colorful stories of pirates and privateers that sailed on these pristine waters while burying their treasures beneath swaying palms majestically protruding like guards over virgin beaches. The likes of Edward Teach and Cofresi have long faded into history along with their tall ships and the men-of-war that aggressively pursued them. Unfortunately these scoundrels have been replaced by 21st century villains whose plunder is not gold or silver or other riches from the new world but narcotics produced in the labs of Colombia with coca leaf from the fields of Ecuador, Bolivia and Peru. This new breed of pirate not only deals in contraband but has expanded its influences to include the financing of terrorist insurrection, kidnapping, money laundering, transport of illegal aliens, and the theft of high value yachts which involves insurance fraud. When pursued, the perpetrators seek not the shelter provided in secluded bays or hidden coves, but through scores of less than honorable lawyers adorned in designer suits using liberal laws to shield their nefarious clients from prosecution. These present day culprits offer not the sometimes historic escapades of pirates of yesteryear but reveal a clear and present danger, not only to the local inhabitants of the area, but a serious threat to the stability of the elected governments of the region. While initially appearing to be an isolated incident related to marine theft and fraud, an ironic twist involves a case where the American Central Intelligence Agency was implicated in a case where they allegedly provided cover in the theft of a high value yacht used to transport narcotics from Cartagena, Colombia. Prior to this incident the CBS news program 60 Minutes exposed another covert CIA operation involving a General in the Venezuelan National Guard who was paid to facilitate the illicit transport of cocaine through Caracas's Maquetia airport to Miami. While not charged or authorized as a law enforcement agency, the CIA has been exposed as a lawless conspirator whose history in the Caribbean and Latin America includes compromising the integrity of elected governments the funding of death squads and before the invasion of Panama, the use of Manual Noriega as an asset. After his unsuccessful and bloody coup to overthrow the elected government of Venezuela in February 1992 Lt. Colonel Hugo Chavez was convicted and jailed. During his incarceration Chavez became a lackey under the wing of the CIA mission in Caracas. Ostensibly to continue the flow of oil from Venezuela's rich reserves to the United States, Chavez, a left-wing socialist was clandestinely recruited and provided money and support that the CIA guaranteed would install him as President of the Republic of Venezuela.

In return for their efforts the CIA wanted Chavez's *cooperation*. The CIA's operation to bring Chavez to power included the recruitment and compromising of the integrity of a number of elected members of the government and a conspiracy that would set into motion a plan to compromise the general officers of country's military. CIA Agent Joseph Velling under the cover as a Commercial Attaché in the American Embassy in Caracas set about a program of destabilization code named Operation Deep Six. The Operation was established to obtain private information of the general officers of the Venezuelan Army, Guardia Nacional, Air Force and Navy. Velling wanted to know the officers private home addresses, confidential cellular telephone numbers, where they kept private bank accounts outside Venezuela, where their children went to school and the names and addresses of mistresses or girl friends, the CIA was also keenly interested in any political leanings they might have. I was made aware of the CIA's interests and activities when Velling contacted me for my assistance and *cooperation*. Between 1991 and 1995 I had been commissioned by the U.S. Coast Guard to assist the Venezuela Navy in restructuring and training of its recently formed Coastguard Command. During this period I worked closely with the Navy's Rear Admiral Enrique Jesus Briceno Garcia who at the time was the Commandant of the Venezuelan Coastguard and the U.S. Coast Guard attaché based in the American Embassy in Caracas. The training program achieved an outstanding level of success and as a result of this success the Venezuelan Coastguard promoted me to the rank of Captain and appointed me Special Policy Advisor of Auxiliary Affairs to the Commandant of the Venezuelan Coastguard. Not to be outdone in 1992 the U.S. Coast Guard also promoted me to the rank of Captain in the U.S. Coast Guard Auxiliary. Normally the U.S. Coast Guard Auxiliary doesn't operate outside of the United States except maybe for those Auxiliary Commodores in Washington who were able to convince the Commandant, maybe con would be a better word, that a trip at taxpayer's expense to Japan or a life boat meeting in Europe would be good for their moral. On the other hand not needing a boost in moral, I personally paid all my expenses to train the Venezuelan Coastguard. In a very short time I had been asked to present training programs at the Venezuelan Naval War College and to provide training to Coastguard and Navy commands throughout the country. In frequently being invited to their homes, professional and personal friendships developed with most of the Generals and Admirals of the Venezuelan armed forces, an accomplishment that had not gone unnoticed by the CIA and the United States Ambassador, Martin Skol. The CIA wanted intelligence on the military forces of Venezuela and wanted me to provide it.

When Velling later contacted me at a Navy League meeting at Roosevelt Roads Naval Station he didn't beat around the bush. Velling said I had been *monitored* on all my visits to Venezuela and they knew of my high level contacts within the military and the respect I had gained leading to my promotion to the rank of Captain in the Para-military Venezuelan Coastguard Auxiliary. He also knew that I was in line for promotion to flag rank (Commodore) in the US Coast Guard Auxiliary. The CIA's proposition was very simple; I would become a CIA-NOC (No Official Cover) *asset* and provide intelligence that the CIA needed concerning the

Venezuelan military, in return they would guarantee my promotion in the U.S. Coast Guard, reimburse the money I had personally spent on the USCG training mission and put me on the payroll through a CIA slush fund Velling said he had access to. As America's National Security wasn't at stake I refused to accept the CIA's assignment to spy on my friends. A short time after refusing the assignment the USCG in Washington closed down the Venezuelan Training Initiative. In the meantime Admiral Enrique Jesus Briceno Garcia had been promoted to the position of Commanding Admiral of the Venezuelan Navy, as he was my friend, I warned him that the CIA were watching and making moves to overthrow the government. A week later I was disenrolled from the Auxiliary and my record of 16 years service to the USCG disappeared. I wrote to the Commandant of the US Coast Guard and to James Woolsey who was then the Director of the CIA, demanding to know why. My letters were firm but nice. The deputy director of the CIA wrote back denying any knowledge of a plan to spy on the Venezuelan military adding that the CIA would never have me thrown out of the Coast Guard for refusing to become a CIA *asset.* The USCG Commandant didn't reply so I wrote to Bill Ecker, a Rear Admiral that I knew personally at headquarters, and who in 1991 had been made Chief of the Auxiliary. RADM Ecker replied telling me that I should reconsider the offer to work with the CIA at the Embassy in Caracas as if I did, all would be well. My response, thanks, but no thanks. The illustrious CIA agent, Joe Velling told me that this was a covert operation to destabilize the government of Venezuela, and that the national security of the United States wasn't involved. I pointed out that I was a naval officer, not a spy. If the USCG and the CIA wanted to install Hugo Chavez as the president of Venezuela, that was their business, but it wouldn't involve me—period. I was not willing to spy on a friendly ally of the United States or my military colleagues and friends in Caracas for any reason including promotion or any amount of money from an illegal CIA slush fund. I subsequently filed a lawsuit against the USCG in 1995 and thanks to my own *deep throat* within the US Attorneys office, I prevailed, but not before the U.S. Attorney had all the case records sealed.

The reason given by US Attorney for sealing the records of the case was for "Reasons of National Security.

On February 8, 2004 the records of Edwin S. Geary v. U.S. Coast Guard (95-323-CV-Lenard) were unsealed. In December 1998 the CIA without my help successfully installed Hugo Chavez as the President of the Republic of Venezuela. Shortly after assuming the presidency Chavez double crossed and turned on his CIA handlers. Chavez publicly challenged United States global interests in giving support to America's enemies including Saddam Hussein, Colonel Muammar Quaddafi and Fidel Castro. The present mission of the CIA is to kill Hugo Chavez. Rather than limiting their activities to intelligence gathering and not meddling in the affairs of friendly governments CIA agents regularly venture well beyond their charter and in some drug trafficking cases have actually become customers of the drug cartels. Spending U.S. tax dollars on inane schemes purportedly conceived to catch the *big guys*. In one case in Venezuela, mindless agents in defiance of the law purchased an estimated $20M of Colombian cocaine, shipped it by land over the porous border between Colombia and Venezuela. After arriving at Caracas airport it was loaded onto a Boeing 707 cargo plane for delivery to Miami. When the DEA got wind of the ludicrous scheme they tried to stop it, but were just a bit too late. The unmarked 707 left Maquetia Airport but didn't go to Miami. The plane and its contents were never seen again. In an effort to compromise a governments integrity or as we have seen in Venezuela, orchestrate the installation of a devious puppet, the CIA working clandestinely with the U.S. Coast Guard has severely damaged the integrity of the United States and hampered the effectiveness of other agencies such as the Defense Intelligence Agency (DIA) for the sake of their own agenda. This covert agenda is withheld from oversight by the Department of State, Congress and the Senate. Much like its secretive budget, the CIA has never been exposed to congressional scrutiny or review by the Senate Committee on Intelligence. Covert CIA support and slush fund financing of narcotics trafficking in South America has revealed government officials in Colombia illegally acquiring yachts which had been reported stolen in the Caribbean (again to ostensibly catch the Big Guys) at the expense of yacht owners and their insurers. With the exception of very limited local law enforcement reports of yacht thefts there is even less of an opportunity of recovery. The impact is being felt not only by residents, but also by shore-based tourists and the yachties that sail with the trades between Trinidad and Belize. On the island of St. Lucia narcotics are frequently offered for sale in the marinas and even on the tennis courts of the leading hotels on the island. One island recently reported 21 stolen boats of the type used by local fisherman, small boats with high powered single or twin outboard engines, of those recovered most were said to have been used to transport narcotics. One can only wonder what number of these cases were secretly financed by the CIA in other abortive schemes as part of their flawed policy in this area known as the *Drug Highway to the States*. In some cases these incidents may have been limited to the individual entrepreneur who believed he could become rich and retire by transporting narcotics to the northern islands of Martinique, Antigua, St. Maarten or the Virgin Islands. However, more and more of this illicit trade is now part of a larger picture that includes organized crime which has penetrated the region and its governments. Insurance companies still continue issuing policies and are paying out thousands of dollars in claims which continue at an alarming rate throughout the Caribbean. A yacht or recreational vessel is an easy target for thieves and in the previously mentioned case of the French Connection II can serve additional needs. Marine theft is considered a high value—low risk crime. Auto theft on a worldwide basis has been closely related to marine theft; yet the values of luxury automobiles with a street value of between $75,000 to $150,000 pales when compared with an ultra modern catamaran that can be worth $500,000 or a second hand 40' to 50' sailing or motor yacht that can fetch $200,000 or more. An automobile has VIN (vehicle identification number) allowing police agencies worldwide to track and trace vehicles through a sophisticated international computer network. With yachts, well that's another story. Once a yacht is stolen and leaves the jurisdiction of the United States they are generally gone, unless a sharp investigator happens to get lucky. As from November 1, 1972 all boats sold in the United States were required to have a hull identification number (HIN). In the United States the HIN is secured by a plate or molded into the transom of the hull on the starboard side, the same number is placed in a hidden location inside the vessel. In the case of a homemade boat it will have a State issued HIN containing the letter Z. As an example a homemade boat registered in California would be issued with a 12 digit HIN that would begin CAZ, in Florida the number would start FLZ. The letter Z behind the state letter ID indicates it's a home-made and a state registered boat. The purpose of the HIN is to deter theft and assist law enforcement in the recovery if the vessel is stolen. In the United States the HIN system is extremely effective and a valuable tool of vessel identification. The alteration of a hull identification number is a felony crime. Outside the United States it's another matter. Thieves can alter the HIN or delete it completely, change the appearance of the vessel, like painting it another color then sell it to an unsuspecting buyer. Without traceable HIN's jet skis stolen in the United States are frequently shipped, sometimes by container loads to operators in Central America, Mexico and the Caribbean. A recent case found that almost 50% of the jet skis in the Dominican Republic had been stolen in the United States. Outside of the United States most coastguards, marine police or customs don't have a clue what the HIN is or what it represents and few have ever received training in the law enforcement use of the HIN. Over the last number of years insurance fraud worldwide has grown at a phenomenal rate, developing into a lucrative business that's the result of very creative criminal minds. This is especially true in Russia and the former eastern block countries. Drug money has made many Russian entrepreneurs wealthy and desirous of the playthings they were denied in the past under the heavy burden of socialism and the communist doctrines. These playthings include sailing and motor yachts usually in the 40' to 50' range, some stolen in the United States and others in the Caribbean have had their appearance and identifiers altered in Colombia or other locations in the area before being sold again. In some cases INTERPOL has found these yachts which are sometimes fitted with secret compartments that are filled with narcotics before being loaded into the holds of Russian or former eastern block cargo ships which then sail to ports in the Mediterranean, Baltic or the Black Sea where they take on a new identity and begin a new life. Neat and clean. The stolen yacht(s) simply disappear forever unless a diligent insurance investigator gets a tip or comes across an identifying mark that warrants a closer look. Marine fraud and theft is a problem that has been around for a number of years, but really started to get out of hand during the 1980's and the reign of the *Cocaine Cowboys*. Because of his commitment and foresight in the early 1990's Major Dave McGillis created and fathered an organization named the National Association of Marine Investigators or *NAMI*. The organization quickly grew to international stature with a growing number of members being drawn from Europe and as far away as Australia. As the director in charge of the international side of the *NAMI* I proposed that our name be changed to the International Association of Marine Investigators, National was soon dropped and the organization became the International Association of Marine Investigators or *IAMI*. The *IAMI* membership is currently made up of insurance investigators, law enforcement and marine surveyors eager to learn more of the intricacies of marine fraud and theft. The organization is now actively involved with advanced educational training programs throughout the world. The *IAMI* has played an important role in successfully bringing together the financial strength of the insurance industry with law enforcement. While focused on marine theft and fraud these forces may also have a positive effect in the deterrence of narcotics trafficking. It's pretty clear that the touted *war on drugs* has been a dismal failure. When one drug delivery route receives attention the drug lords simply switch to another. In spite of politically anointed drug czars, other potentates and media rivalry between a number of federal agencies competing for the billions being spent on the *war*, Law enforcement reports that drug seizures amount to only about 5% of what is shipped. But that of course doesn't include narcotics that the CIA attempts to deliver with purchases from its slush fund.

The author with Admiral Jesus Enrique Briceno Garcia
Commanding Admiral of the Venezuelan Navy

Rear Admiral Martin Fossa, Commandant of the
Venezuelan Coastguard (left) The author (center)
Venezuelan Coastguard Auxiliary aide (right)

Venezuelan Coastguard training missions were also carried out at U.S. Coast Guard Base San Juan

Maritime Experts and the Federal Rules of Evidence

Most dictionaries describes ex-pert—*n* one who is very skillful or well-informed in some special field. Prior to 1993, under Rule 702 testimony of Experts, those individuals who were accepted as an expert generally were those who could demonstrate a high degree of proficiency based on scientific, technical, or other specialized knowledge that would assist the trier of fact to understand the evidence or to determine a fact in issue. A witness qualified as an expert by knowledge, skill, experience, training or education, was permitted to testify thereto in the form of an opinion or otherwise, if (1) the testimony is based upon sufficient facts or data, (2) the testimony is the product of reliable principles and methods, and (3) the witness has applied the principles and reliably to the facts of the case. Two U.S. Supreme Court cases and the recent amendment of Rule 702 of the Federal Rules of Evidence have significantly changed the perspective and position in federal court cases of all testifying experts. The first case to impact the perception of experts was the 1993 decision of Daubert v. Merrel Dow Pharmaceuticals Inc., 509 U.S. 579. Daubert provided a broad check-list of conditions for trial courts to apply in accessing the reliability of scientific expert testimony, which included whether the expert's theory or techniques could be tested or whether it had been tested. This asked if the expert's theory could be challenged in some objective sense, or is it simply a subjective, conclusory approach that cannot be reasonably assessed for reliability. Another element is whether the theory or methodology has been subject to peer review and publication and what is the known or possible rate of error of the technique or theory when applied. Daubert also brought forward the question of whether the theory or technique had been generally accepted by the scientific community. Contradictory results were apparent in the circuit courts as to whether the Daubert decision applied to non-scientific evidence; this question was clearly addressed and answered by the U.S. Supreme Court in its decision in the Kumho Tire Company, Limited v. Carmichael, 526 U.S. 137 (1999) which acknowledged that the factors were to be considered for all experts, not just scientific experts.

The court established that Daubert was not to be applied automatically, but rather that the reliability and methodological requirements of Daubert were essential to any determination of admissibility of expert evidence. In concert with the Kumho decision, the trial judge as the gate-keeper would have substantial latitude in making the final decision in assessing the reliability of non-scientific expert testimony. To remove all questions concerning the applicability of the factors and the gate-keeping role of the trial judges, the Federal Rules of Evidence were changed effective 1 December 2000.

Rule 701—Opinion Testimony by Lay Witnesses: States that if a witness is not testifying, as an expert, the witness testimony in the form of an opinion or inference is limited to those opinions or inferences that are (1) rationally based on the perception of the witness, (2) helpful to provide a clear understanding of the witness' testimony or the determination of a fact in issue, (3) not based on scientific, technical or other specialized knowledge within the scope of Rule 702.

Rule 702—Testimony by Experts: If scientific, technical, or other specialized knowledge will assist the trier of fact to understand the evidence or to determine a fact in issue, a witness qualified as an expert by knowledge, skill, experience, training or education, may testify thereto in the form of an opinion or otherwise, if (1.) the testimony is based upon sufficient facts or data, (2) the testimony is the product of reliable principles and methods, and (3) the witness has applied the principles and methods reliably to the facts of the case.

Rule 703 Bases of Opinion Testimony by Experts: The facts or data in the particular case upon which an expert bases an opinion or inference may be those perceived by or made known to the expert at or before the hearing. If of a type reasonably relied upon by experts in the particular field in forming opinions or inference upon the subject, the facts or data need not be admissible in evidence in order for the opinion or inference to be admitted. Facts or data that are otherwise inadmissible shall not be disclosed to the jury by the proponent of the opinion or inference unless the court determines that their probative value in assisting the jury to evaluate the expert's opinion substantially outweighs the prejudicial effect. Since the Daubert decision all trial court judges are taking a closer look at the basis of expert testimony and taking steps to exclude a high proportion.

Citing the Daubert case Chief Justice William Rehnquist stated, "The focus, of course, must be solely on principles and methodology, not on the conclusions they generate." In addition to specific time limits and requirements for expert's reports, under Rule 26 of the Federal Rules of Civil Procedure the expert is charged with providing a report that includes, but not limited to (a) a complete statement of all opinions, (b) the basis and supporting reasons for his or her opinions. (c) the full supporting data and other information considered by the expert in forming his or her opinion, (d) all supporting documentation and certificates in support of the expert's qualifications, (e) a list and preferably copies of all technical publications authored by the expert within the last 10 years, (t) a description and documentation of the compensation paid and/or to be paid for the research, study and testimony, and (g) a detailed list of other cases in which the expert has testified in deposition and trial over the preceding four years. Entering the arena of the expert witness can be a daunting task. The role of the expert is to inform and educate without bias or prejudice. Much like the professional thespian an expert must always consider the courtroom as a theater of dignity and respect. The expert is just one of the players who must present his facts and findings and clearly articulate his opinion. Display or arrive at a conclusion with prejudice or bias and the case will surely be lost However. even before the proceedings begin. The first test of the emerging expert's real or perceived qualifications will initially be determined by the defense or plaintiffs lawyers who will question and challenge the experts' knowledge, skill, experience, training and education. 30 years crawling around the holds of ships or the bilge's of yachts may be admirable and provide some level of basic knowledge and experience, but may be deficient and expose a critical void in professional training and education. Without question these issues that will ultimately be addressed by the trial judge. This knowledge and experience may also be inconsequential and of little value unless supported by thorough and comprehensive training and continuing education from recognized institutions of advanced learning. Knowledge may be power, but without the supporting certificates to prove it, the trial judge or gate-keeper will quickly close the gate bringing an immediate end to a career, before it even had a chance to start. Continuing educational certificates from Class Societies and other professional organizations such as the Society of Naval Architects and Marine Engineers, the National Association of Marine Surveyors and the Society of Accredited Marine Surveyors in the USA, the Yacht Designers and Surveyors Association and the Royal Institution of Naval Architects in the UK are fundamental in establishing maritime credibility. Another valuable credential, critical in valuation issues are that of Accredited Senior Appraiser status from the American Society of Appraisers in Washington, D.C. At the present time throughout the world there are but 11 Accredited Senior Appraisers of yachts, 14 who hold ASA certification of commercial vessels and 2 who hold ASA designation for both yachts and commercial vessels. When it comes to maritime insurance fraud, one only need consider the Association of Certified Fraud Examiners of Austin, Texas. The Bottom Line: For those who qualify and are interested in adding Expert Witness to their curriculum vitae the effort will provide valuable expertise to the judiciary, while at the same time be intellectually challenging and personally rewarding. A word of caution; even though an assignment may appear financially appealing, an expert should never accept a case that is beyond his or her expertise. A review of the case summary or the pleadings will provide the expert with a determination of the issues before the assignment is accepted. While the individual's normal fee schedule may apply for research and preparation, depositions and courtroom appearance are generally charged at a fixed rate, portal-to-portal, and can vary from $1,000.00 to $1,500.00 per day or more depending on the experts' professional qualifications. However, it's an unfortunate fact that from time to time unscrupulous lawyers will attempt to obtain expert testimony under Rule 701—Opinion Testimony by a Lay Witness can be as low as $35.00. Fortunately the Federal Rules have made provisions for such scurrilous conduct. It is the prerogative and the right of a truly qualified expert to lodge an appeal with the presiding trial judge under Rule 706(b) Compensation; "In other civil actions and proceedings the compensation shall be paid by the parties in such proportion and as such time as the court directs, and thereafter charged in like manner as other costs." If called as a lay witness, then any subpoena as such must be strictly adhered to, if however the court deems the witness to be an expert, he or she is entitled to reasonable expenses and their normal expert fees. Distances and location of scheduled appearances are considerations that must be factored into the equation. If say, the expert is asked to testify in the Southern District of New York and they might live in Dallas, the expert must reach an agreement with the client as to when the clock starts ticking. In most cases professional services as an expert are charged portal-to-portal, that is, when you depart until such time as you return. After agreeing to accept the assignment as an expert in the case, one should calculate approximately how much research and preparation time will be needed, where and how many depositions he or she might be required to attend and the estimated number of days in trial. The expert's appearance at a deposition or trial always requires that the lawyer *prepare the witness*. Depending on the complexity of the case this preparation time could range from one to a number of hours and is chargeable time. Any lawyer or expert, regardless of their experience, who believes pre-appearance preparation isn't necessary, is doomed to failure. The expert should draft a retainer agreement that recites specifically what is required and when and where you will be asked to do it. After insuring that your policy covering errors & omissions insurance is currently in effect, present the retainer agreement along with an invoice to the lawyer for execution and payment.

Not until the retainer agreement is signed and returned with the agreed payment should the case be accepted. If counsel should hesitate at paying a retainer before the conflict commences, it may be a clear indication that fees and expenses won't be paid during the heat of battle or after the last salvo has been fired. With the proper credentials, sound preparation and research, professional presentation in the courtroom and without the heart-burn of maybe collecting your fees and expenses, the expert witness is in an enviable position. However, as all experts know he or she will only be remembered by the results of their last case.

Good-bye My Love

A story based on actual events

Sam was a tall, handsome and energetic man who belied his true age of 63. He was trim, athletic and was an avid sailor. After completing his studies at Columbia and graduating cum laude, he went directly to the Navy and rose rapidly to the rank of Captain. Shortly after his promotion he met and married the daughter of his Commanding Officer at the Alameda Naval Air Station in Oakland, California. Ms. Beverly Adams was a beautiful bride and complimented the young naval officer with her dignified grace and elegant charm obtained during her education in Switzerland and at Roedean in England. The two had traveled extensively during Sam's naval career and had enjoyed the luxuries afforded to naval officers of command rank. The years had been good to Sam and Bev and prudent investments made after the untimely death of Bev's parents, had seen her large inheritance grow ten fold. The only thing missing were the children that Sam so badly wanted, but Bev couldn't provide due to the abortion she had as a young teenager. As the plane touched down at Beef Island in Tortola in the British Virgin Islands, both Sam and Bev were captivated by the beauty of the crystal blue water and white sand beaches that fringes the small islands and cays of this tropical paradise. The taxi ride from the airport took Captain and Mrs. Brown over the Queen Elizabeth II Bridge past the old Go Vacations Charter Base through the settlement of East End to the rolling hills overlooking Road Harbour and the city of Road Town. As they walked down the dock to the *Spirit*, they saw Marty Gold and Inga Wolfson, their crew for the delivery of the *Spirit* back to her home port of Miami. Marty and Inga had known Sam and Bev for over thirty years and had been neighbors of the Browns in Falmouth, Massachusetts. Marty had retired a few years back after 20 years as a lawyer and had met Inga when she was a flight attendant with the Scandinavian Airlines System. Inga had moved in with Marty when she was transferred to the SAS Base at JFK in New York. "Hi Marty, hello Inga been on board yet?" "No Sam, we just got here", replied Marty. "We had to take the Bomba Charger from St. Thomas because we missed the last Air BVI flight to Beef".

The four walked down the dock to the 43 foot sailboat *Spirit* and went aboard as the sun began to set on this warm winter day in the Caribbean. It hadn't been that long when Sam remembered the strong wind that was driving heavy drifts of snow across the road as he had driven the few miles into the suburbs of Boston. The offices of Fidelity Insurance were cold but the warmth of the receptionist brought a broad smile to Sam's face. "Can I help you, Sir?" "Yes, I've got an appointment with Bob Delgado about some life insurance". "Just a moment please", the girl then dialed a number, "Mr. Delgado, I have a gentleman here to see you, he says you are expecting him. Your name sir, "Sam Brown", replied Sam. "Of course, yes Mr. Delgado—you may go in Mr. Brown." The papers seemed endless, form after form. "OK, Mr. Brown that's one million each term life for you and Mrs. Brown. The medicals are fine and we'll get the policies to you the early part of next week". "No need to mail them to me, I'll be in Boston next Thursday and I'll stop by and collect them". Sam hoped that the Insurance agent hadn't noticed his anxiety. It had taken him weeks to get Bev's medical records and perfect her signature to a point that it wouldn't be questioned on the application. He didn't want to blow the whole thing if Bev saw an insurance policy on her life; but also didn't want the policies mailed to his home in case Bev got to the mail before him. Sam started to perspire in an office that was a cold 60 degrees. Over a period of four years he had carefully planned the death of his wife and now everything was falling into place. Rod Sheldon was a Podiatrist in Boston and owned a 43 foot ketch that was in charter service in the Virgin Islands. During the previous summer Rod had invited Sam and Bev out to Newport to sail with him on a boat he had chartered and mentioned that he planned to bring the *Spirit* back to Newport the following season because he had been unhappy with the charter company and their seemingly endless bills for repairs. Sam had jumped at the chance to act as the delivery skipper. The thought of an ocean voyage with a woman he had grown to hate would present the opportunity for the perfect crime. The childless couple had first been happy in the early days of their marriage, but what should have been a perfect union soon fell apart. Sam, however, had never forgiven Bev for not telling him she couldn't have children until a after they were married. They both began to drink heavily and Sam had numerous affairs between drinking binges that sometimes lasted days on end.

Many times Sam had been cautioned by his navy superiors about reporting for duty while appearing to be under the influence, but his wit, charm and an Admiral for a father-in-law had always kept him clear of harms way or a Court Martial. At one point Sam thought seriously of divorcing Bev, but when her parents died and left their only offspring an accumulated $9.8 million dollars, he no longer thought of divorce but how he could get rid of the "wicked witch of the west" and keep the entire inheritance to himself. The million dollar life policy he had purchased on Bev's life was simply the frosting on the cake. His scheme was simple. He'd been careful in his planning, credited to his training at the Naval Academy; he had the time, a boat to sink and been able to organize a crew that knew them both and who could attest to Bev's accidental death. Marty and Inga fitted this need perfectly. For Bev's last few days on earth like any accomplished thespian Sam would carefully set the stage for his approaching performance. He'd be a kind, gentle and loving husband for the world and his crew to see. Sam smiled as he pondered over the charts and carefully plotted the trip from the Virgins North to Florida. Muttering to himself he carefully evaluated his options in looking at the various potential ports of call. First stop maybe Mayaguana; he thought, yes, that's good, small population and few other boats to contend with. I'll say the stop was needed for emergency repairs. Let's see, I'll disconnect the navigation lights and the compass lights and add a touch of saw dust in the fuel tank. That should do it. Damn, the VHF radio and flares, those have got to go, we don't want any do-gooders coming to our rescue. As Sam's finger moved up the chart, he momentary looked at the names of the various islands and cays. Yes, that looks good, past Seal Cays, midway between West Caicos and Little Inagua and then straight to Abraham's Bay on Mayaguana. His mind was running like a computer, figuring distances, location of reefs and the chance of rescue if something went wrong. If he pressed on to the Exumas, there were more people and if Bev didn't drown right away she might be rescued, also there would be more cruising boats in the area that might come to their assistance. That leaves either Acklins Island or Diana Reef off Fortune Island south of Long Cay. The chart showed that the reef south west of Acklins would be perfect. The reef had shallow water out about 3 miles and a sparse population. After a few calls he found that Air Bahamas had flights to and from Acklins on Wednesday and Saturdays. With careful planning he could carry out the perfect crime step ashore and be on his way home within 24 hours as a single man with a net worth of over $11 million dollars. "Sam, this thing's a peace of shit". Marty said looking at the cockpit of the boat. "Christ, look at the sails, they're stained and look like they're a 100 years old."

Marty had been a weekend sailor on the Chesapeake and had a pretty good knowledge of boats, he was obviously not impressed with the *Spirit*. The boat also had foul odors coming up from the bilges and heads that probably hadn't been properly flushed or cleaned for a year. After a gallant attempt to clean the *Spirit* they all agreed they'd spend their last night in Tortola at Village Cay. After a number of Margaritas, a bountiful meal and two bottles of great Beaujolais at Spaghetti Junction a small bistro across the road, they staggered back to their rooms at Village Cay. Sam had made an extra effort to get two of the "B" rooms that face the town, instead of the more expensive "A" rooms that overlook the marina. After Bev had fallen into drunken slumber and began her normal snoring, Sam slipped into his clothes and made his way to the dock and the *Spirit*. The little ketch didn't look half bad in the dim lights of the marina as she gently tugged at her frayed mooring lines in anticipation of fleeing the Virgins for the high seas. Sam unfurled the jib and pulled the main sail open looking closely at the clew, head and other vital parts of the sails. The running rigging looked tired but Sam felt certain that it would hold up for one last voyage. The standing rigging and all the swedge fittings holding the wire in place were badly rusted, but it was a downhill run with following seas and hopefully the wind at their backs. Sam was confident that if he didn't push the *Spirit* the rig should hold together for at least one more week. Finishing his cursory inspection he stowed the main and used the roller furling to return the jib. Down below he found the wires to the panel switch for the running lights were badly corroded; a light tug pulled them loose. The passage would be both night and day and a compass light might be helpful, but he'd rely on his expertise in celestial navigation. He pulled the small wires for the compass light and they came apart in his hand. The VHF radio wouldn't work when he turned it on because the fuse was blown; replacing the fuse and to be sure it wouldn't work he loosened the coaxial antenna wire and cut the end that made contact with the female receptacle. He found four ocean service life jackets stuffed under the forward vee berth, wet from bilge water and musty from the lack of ventilation, he secreted the best one in a cockpit locker and jammed the rest back into their mildewed compartment. Three flares swollen from water were lying beneath the galley sink. After closing up the boat Sam strolled back to his room laughing as he read a Trip Survey performed for the owner by a local surveyor that described the *Spirit* in good condition, fully found and ready for sea. The next morning, Marty and Inga were in the restaurant having breakfast when Sam and Bev came down.

Small talk was exchanged, then it was decided that Marty and Inga would pick up the last provisions at Bobby's Supermarket before clearing out with customs and immigration before departing. Sam was insistent that they sail at least by noon, not because he had to leave in daylight, but for no other reason than to prevent his crew from finding out they had no compass or navigation lights. The lines of the *Spirit* were cast off at 11:30 a.m. With winds of 15 knots the *Spirit* was soon moving briskly in the open seas. At about 7:00 p.m. in the failing light, Sam asked Inga, to go below and turn on the navigation lights. "Sam, is it the one that says "NAV"? "Yes Inga, switch it on", responded Sam. "Marty please, help her out", Sam called out to his mate who had been napping on the foredeck. From down below Marty called to Sam, "the switch is on.". "Marty take a look to see if the fuse is blown." "Nope, the fuse is ok, I'll check the bulbs". Marty began looking for a flashlight and eventually found a plastic one that emitted about as much light as the glow of hot coals. "Bulbs are ok maybe the wires are broken." "Marty not to worry, don't forget I taught celestial navigation at the academy, I'll steer by the stars tonight and we'll fix them in the morning". Marty, Inga and Bev could not see the small smile that filled Sam's face. The sun slowly came up on the horizon as Sam rubbed the sleep from his eyes. The forward cabin was now quiet with Marty and Inga fast asleep. During the night Sam had heard Inga groaning as Marty had obviously brought her to numerous peaks of orgasmic sensation. Both must have been exhausted by the time they finished and rolled over in blissful serenity. Lucky bastard as Sam thought of his wife's idea that sex was something to be undertaken at regular intervals of maybe once a month. Once the dust had settled and he received his money the first thing that he would schedule was a visit to Jackie O's in Acapulco, where he would satisfy 10 years of married abstinence with the first comer. And he told himself that he didn't care if it was a matron from Milwaukee or a hooker from the Hyatt. The gentle roll of the boat moving through the turquoise seas and gentle breeze brushing his face made him close his eyes and dream of the future, his future. "God Damn it", the words rang through the rigging. "Damn, this frigging stove doesn't work", shouted Marty through the open hatch. "Did you pump it Marty? Alcohol stoves need to be pumped before they work", replied Sam. Running up the steps Inga shouted, "Sam "We're on fire, we're on fire!" the fearful shriek penetrated the once serene environment. "Sam, come quickly the curtains are on fire". When Marty pumped the stove he had apparently done so with the valve open, when he put a match to the burner, it flared up igniting the curtains. "Where's the fire extinguisher?" "I don't know, grab a bucket of water and throw it over the curtains", Sam said placing Inga's hands on the ships wheel.

It took a little more than an hour to clean up the mess and dry the stove so they could fix coffee and a spartan breakfast of cold cereal and soggy bread. Inga had been at the wheel while Sam and Marty dealt with the fire and its aftermath of charred cupboards and burnt rayon. As Sam came back up on deck, he sensed something was wrong. "Damn it, the sun's on the starboard side. Inga, what the hell have you done we've turned 180 degrees and put us on a course back to the Virgin Islands!" "Oh, sorry Sam, it's just with all the confusion…" "Oh, forget it", Sam said rolling his eyes looking to the clouds as he put the boat back on course. Three days later as the *Spirit* rounded the headland and made its way towards the open bay that Mayaguana called its harbour, Sam pressed the start button to fire up the Perkins diesel, the only response was subdued click. "Christ Marty, looks like we've got dead batteries." I'll bring her around and when she's pointing into the wind, drop the hook". Sam made a wide swing about a mile from the shore when he heard the clang and rattle of the anchor as its chain fed out over the bow roller. After the anchor was secured, he furled the jib and stowed the main, leaving the mizzen in place to stabilize the boat while she swung in the offshore breeze. Bev had been very quiet the last 24 hours and Sam guessed she had her nose stuck into a book. Sam thought of the many times they had gone to bed and he had exerted considerable effort in trying to arouse his wife only to be told that she wanted to read. The jokes and comments he had been aware of at the officers club about his 100 lb. 5'2" wife who was endowed with a bosom that if activated could feed the entire Pacific fleet always bothered him. After many years of infrequent penetration of her innermost parts and sterile fondling of her breasts, Sam had lost interest. A moment later Bev climbed the companionway steps from the aft cabin asking, "Are we there yet?" Turning, Sam said: "We're at Mayaguana in the lower Bahamas;

we'll stop here and try to fix the lights and try to get someone to charge the batteries. We might even be able to get the stove working". The next few hours had Marty rowing to shore in the badly leaking Avon inflatable in an effort to find some place to charge the two 6D batteries. In the meantime Sam gave the appearance of trying to fix the navigation lights. The anchorage was deserted with only a few small buildings visible in the distance. Inga and Bev weren't really close friends but had known each other more as acquaintances. They hadn't said too much to one another since leaving Road Town, but once the boat stopped moving and was swinging on the hook Inga and Bev had been like two hens cackling away on the foredeck.

Inga in true Danish fashion had stripped off her clothes and was sitting cross legged leaning against the main mast. The 55 year old Bev who felt nudity had no place in modern society, but obviously influenced by her younger shipmate was now laying flat on her back covered only by a thin layer of tanning cream. Sam busied himself below deck, not repairing things but just looking around. The forward cabin contained Marty's clothes and a very expensive Nikon camera. Inga's bag revealed some adult toys and two sets of extra batteries. Sam laughed and thought to himself, I guess the *toys* were insurance in case Marty couldn't perform Inga could get herself off mechanically. Considering their activity last night this didn't appear to be a problem that Inga would experience. As Sam continued his sweep through the *Spirit*, he found the forward seacocks were leaking and the bilges around the mast step already had about a foot of water in them. The boat had two bilge pumps that with a capacity of 750 gallons per hour may have been better suited for a fish tank in someone's home. The forward pump didn't work, but after reconnecting the ground wire, Sam got it working. He wanted to lose the boat and kill his wife but only on his schedule. He definitely didn't want a premature flooding that he couldn't control. Even though Sam had put sawdust in the fuel tank to foul the engine, it appears that it wasn't necessary because the ships batteries wouldn't hold a charge anyway. About five hours later, Marty returned to the boat. It was about 1:00 p.m. and they all prepared to have some lunch. The preparation of lunch proved to be an interesting experience when it was found that at some point the refrigeration on the boat had stopped working the food while not totally bad was getting warm. The refrigeration system got its power from the batteries which were charged by the engine alternator. With the batteries being dead they had been unable to run the engine so the refrigeration had drained what power was left in the batteries something Sam hadn't planned on. The milk had to be thrown away and the four devoured what was left of the salami and cheddar cheese. The chicken and meat they had planned to cook during the voyage was fed to the fish. Over their meager lunch they discussed the remainder of the voyage and living off canned goods and soda crackers. "Sam, I know you're an expert in navigation, but I understand these waters are pretty dangerous night and day. The fellow who tried to help me with the batteries said we should stay here tonight and leave in the morning. He said to try and pass Acklin's Island at night is very dangerous and a lot of boats end up on the reef. He suggested that we leave at first light and take the outside passage directly to San Salvador".

Marty had a grim look in his face. Sam smiled. "Marty, I've taken destroyers with a 35' draft through the Marianas and most of the South Pacific. I'm sure I can take a 43' sailboat with 5' draft through a five mile channel in the Bahamas, trust me". "But Sam, we have no engine, no batteries, no compass or navigation lights in a boat that seems to be rapidly falling apart". Marty appeared distraught. "Marty, I want to be home by New Years. If we go on the outside we'll lose two days in this hulk". Sam was adamant that no one was going to change his very carefully laid plans. About 4:00 p.m. Marty and Inga struggled with the anchor and after bringing it up, stowed it carefully in the foredeck locker. Bev was reading in the cockpit and as the sails filled, went below to the aft cabin. The boat heeled over and started to pound as she moved from the protected lee of the island. Two frigate birds played tag with the wind scoop and a group of dolphins moved from side to side in front of the bow. Marty offered to take the helm and steer the first watch and Sam agreed. Sam didn't mind Marty taking the helm for a few hours but later would insist to steer the final leg towards Acklins Island. Sam wanted to be certain the *Spirit* would ground on the reef at the right time and the right place. Up until 10:00 p.m. Sam kept watch on the stars and every now and then, had Marty alter his course alternatively from to port and starboard to hold his bearing. When he was relieved Marty went below to obviously play games with his Danish Delight. Sam looked at his watch and the glow of the dial told him that within 4 hours, he would be ready to make an 80° turn to port and drive the *Spirit* onto the reef at Acklins Island.

◆   ◆   ◆

The first indication of shallow water was the loud scrapping of the keel as the *Spirit* slid over the first coral head. As the forward part of the full keel struck the reef the bow dipped and a wave washed over the foredeck flooding the forward cabin through the open hatch. The *Spirit* then made a violent roll to starboard and crashed against a coral head that was only a few feet below the surface; the roll caused the rudder blade to jam leaving the boat with no steerage. The *Spirit* wedged herself between two coral heads and in the blackness of the night was being pounded to death by the raging seas. The sails were flaying themselves against the rigging which was now emitting a high pitch whine as the wind increased. Marty and Inga drenched by the water that came through the forward hatch made their way through the knee deep water and the debris that now littered the main salon.

Marty's shoulder had either been broken or dislocated when he had fallen from the bunk. Inga hadn't been hurt but was hysterical. Slowly the two made their way to the cockpit. In the darkness, Sam could hear them but could only see a faint outline of their form. Marty yelled in pain as he was thrown against the steering pedestal as the *Spirit* rolled again this time heeling to port, the port rail was awash with water filling the cockpit. Sam shouted toward the direction of the aft cabin "Bev, Bev, are you ok?" "Sam, I've hurt my back. Help me, help me please", cried Mrs. Brown, Sam felt his way down the companionway and reached his wife who had been thrown to the corner of the cabin near the aft head. She screamed as he grabbed her arm trying to pull her diminutive body towards him. "Bev, you've got to get up to the cockpit in case the hull breaks up and fills the cabin with water. The rudder had broken off and water was now entering the hull through the open shaft log. Hang on to me!" Sam screamed. Sam's mind was racing, just my luck, the stupid bitch will stay down here, end up injured, but not dead and I'll be stuck with her forever in some nursing home. In what seemed like an eternity, Sam was able to pull his wife up to the cockpit which was continually being battered by the wave action of the angry seas. Sam couldn't see anything clearly, but could feel the upper lifeline and the gate that were still above water. Bev's nails griped her husband's arm piercing the skin. The water was cold and the wind chilled it even further. The salt was burning Sam's eyes and his muscles ached with the strain. Bev was tiring as Sam felt her grip loosen. Sam moved his hand along the starboard gate until he felt the gooseneck fitting that connected the lifeline to the gate. He gently slipped off the safety catch, the lifeline remained connected, but with a sudden jerk he knew it would go free. He pulled Bev up so her back was against the gate. Sam grabbed her right hand and told her to hold tightly to the lifeline gate. Her body seemed cold and the once strong grasp had become limp. "Marty, have you got the life jackets? Try and get one for Bev Sam shouted into the darkness. Marty didn't know where the life jackets were as he'd never looked or previously been asked for them. Sam on the other hand had put on the tattered remains of the best one he had found on board and previously put in the port cockpit locker. Marty began shouting, "Where are the lifejackets. Sam shouted back, "Below the forward v-berth, the v-berth" Marty found them and in the darkness passing one to Sam which he quickly put on Bev. Her body lay motionless against the lifeline supported by Sam's arm; Bev was moaning and faintly repeating, "Sam, Sam, Sam."

With a deafening roar the next large wave crashed against the *Spirit* and with a shuddering movement rolled her from a port list to starboard totally submerging the starboard rail. Sam released his hold on Bev and with a slight push pressed her against the gated lifeline which quickly released itself. Good-bye my love, Sam gently whispered as Bev's body disappeared into the black sea. Sam waited a few moments and then yelled "My God, Bev's been thrown over board!" He repeated it a couple of times to make certain that his calls were heard by Marty and Inga. "I'm going in after her!" shouted Sam in the most convincing voice possible. "Don't be a fool, you'll get killed, stay with the boat. She's got a lifejacket on and will be blown to shore. Once it gets light, we can see where we are and then we'll probably find Bev sitting on the beach." Marty responded yelling like a madman with fear in his voice. Sam smiled to himself yelling, "OK, OK, are you guys alright?" Sam smiled again as he thought about where they were; about 15 W.—22 N, two miles from the southern tip of Acklins Island, population 600. Saturdays and Wednesdays Bahamas Air flies from Acklins to Nassau, it's now probably about 3:00AM Wednesday morning, sunrise at 0617—maybe an hour or so to the beach, a good breakfast, fill out the police report with plenty of time to catch today's flight at 2:15PM to Nassau.

◆   ◆   ◆

They were all cold from being soaked and from having to hang on to the steering pedestal in the strong winds and seas that continued to pound the *Spirit*. The keel had obviously come off and the lower section of the hull ground to a point where only the decks and upper part of the hull resembled a boat. The *Spirit* had been pushed over the outer reef and the wreck was now well inside a small bay, wedged between at least two coral heads. In the early morning light they could see that the water around them was an underwater forest of coral heads situated in depths ranging from 5' to about 8'. Marty was next to useless because of his injured shoulder, so Sam and Inga unlashed the Avon inflatable and pushed it over the side. The inflatable bounced and thrashed about in the short choppy seas that were still sweeping along the hull. One by one, Inga, Marty and Sam slipped into the partially inflated Avon as the dinghy was blown away from the *Spirit* towards the beach off in the distance. Because of the wind and waves all three occupants held on tightly. As they drifted towards the beach now less than two miles away the short choppy seas soon smoothed to a long rolling swell. The three castaways laid their heads back and closed their eyes. It could have been hours but eventually the small boat reached the beach and slid to a stop on the sand. The three exhausted occupants struggled to their feet and walked to the edge of the green turtle grass and dropped to their knees.

Police Constable Jeremy Romney had been on an early morning patrol of southern shore of Acklins Island, when off in the distance he first saw the sails of the *Spirit*. PC Romney at first hadn't given much thought to seeing the sails as many boats frequently pass Acklins Island on their passages between the West Indies and Miami. The sails were blowing in the wind, but the boat wasn't moving. Romney took out his binoculars and could see that the yacht wasn't moving because it was grounded inside the reef.

◆   ◆   ◆

After being washed ashore Bev Brown's body was found by a local fisherman in a cove near a small settlement. After driving the trio back to his home which served as the police station and taking their statements, PC Romney said, "I'm sorry Mr. Brown, but we need to have Nassau's permission for you to leave and take the body back to the States", PC Romney was adamant in his obligations to conform to the regulations, "But the Bahamas Air flight leaves at 2:15 today, there's no reason why we can't be on it", pleaded Sam. He was not happy to learn of the delay needed for Nassau to provide official permission for Bev's body to be flown out of Acklins; this meant he couldn't leave either. Marty and Inga would be permitted to leave, but Sam would have to remain until approval was received from the coroner's office in Nassau. The delay was not in his plan.

◆   ◆   ◆

Two days later the small single engine Comanche that Sam had chartered out of Fort Lauderdale pulled to a stop in front of the small building that Acklins Island called its airport terminal. The removal of the aft seats had allowed enough room for the pine box that a local carpenter had assembled to serve as Bev's coffin to be wedged into the aft part of the fuselage.

◆   ◆   ◆

When the U.S. Coast Guard later located the wreckage of the chartered Comanche it was lying in only about four feet of water. It appeared the undercarriage had struck a coral head when the engine failed and the pilot had attempted to land in the shallow water a short distance offshore. The pilot had been killed on impact. The passenger sitting in the right hand seat was later identified as Samuel Brown a retired naval officer from the United States. His death, however, was not from impact or drowning but from decapitation. The casket that was in the aft part of the aircraft had catapulted forward on impact and neatly separated Sam's head from his body.

Some weeks later, the insurance company had agreed to sell the remains of the wreck of the *Spirit* to PC Romney for one dollar. In return he could remove anything of value and take responsibility for removing the wreck. In the course of stripping the wreck of her hatches, masts, rigging and gear, PC Romney found a diary carefully enclosed in a Zip-Loc bag in the aft cabin. The gold leaf lettering on the front the small book indicated, Diary of Beverly Brown. The entries were mostly of her parents and travels as the wife of an officer in the United States Navy, however, the last few pages included entries of her concern that her husband may attempt to take her life. PC Romney then read a note that immediately caught his attention. The entry read, "Delgado's secretary called to confirm that I had received a copy of my life insurance policy issued by the Fidelity Life Insurance Co. of Boston, Mass. Sam has purchased a life insurance policy on my life for one million dollars with a double indemnity clause." While the Police Constable had thought it strange that Samuel Brown had not demonstrated any noticeable remorse in the death of his wife and was more concerned in how soon he could leave Acklins, he had always viewed the death with suspicion, Considering that Sam Brown had survived when the boat had struck the reef, but was decapitated when the plane had crashed, he smiled at the thought of who might have actually killed who. Closing his eyes PC Romney put the diary back on his desk and gently lay back in his chair.

Acknowledgments

Writing a book is a bit like setting off on a voyage. The charts may help you navigate the perilous waters but it's the skipper much like the writer, who ultimately has to accurately convey the events of the passage in his log. I am indebted to my friend and eminent novelist and the father of the late Myles J. Tralins, Robert J. Tralins who encouraged me to undertake the passage which resulted in the creation of 'Gotcha'. To my wife Gabriele to whom I am greatly indebted for her tireless efforts and patience in diligently proof reading the many drafts of the manuscript. To Captain Nicholas Goschenko, and the officers, men and women of the Venezuelan Navy and Coastguard who provided support, encouragement and protection while I was in the crosshairs of the Central Intelligence Agency.

Gabriele, Charlie and Christina

The Officer's Club at Coastguard Headquarters

About the Author

Captain E.S. Geary has appeared as an expert in admiralty and maritime cases in Federal, State & local jurisdictions throughout the USA and Europe, amongst other credentials and qualifications, he holds a US Coast Guard masters license for commercial vessels, was formally the USCG Department Chief—Pan American Auxiliary Liaison and Senior Policy Advisor to the Commandant of the Venezuelan Coastguard. He holds a masters degree (magna cum laude) in Criminal Justice Management, is a Certified Fraud Examiner, Marine Loss Adjuster, member of the American Boat and Yacht Council, American Society of Appraisers and Accredited Senior Appraiser of Yachts & Ships, a Licensed & Registered Professional Engineer, a Fellow of the Institution of Diagnostic Engineers (UK), IRCA Certificated ISO 9001:2000 & ISM Code Internal Auditor, member of the Yacht, Designers & Surveyors Association (UK), authorized Nautical Surveyor approved to carry out work for the United Kingdom Maritime and Coastguard Agency, member of the Society of Naval Architects and Marine Engineers (USA) and The American Society of Naval Engineers, member and past Director of the International Association of Marine Investigators who named him the 1996 Marine Investigator of the Year.

0-595-32740-0

CPSIA information can be obtained at www.ICGtesting.com
Printed in the USA
LVOW11s1545220915

455237LV00002B/385/P

9 780595 327409